A Short History
of

Clan Stewart of Appin

1463 -1752

AND IT'S UNFAILING LOYALTY TO

THE ROYAL HOUSE OF STEWART

by

Michael Starforth, M.A.(Oxon.)

advised by Stuart and Yvonne Carmichael

First published in 1997 by
Appin Historical Society
℅ Dunvegan, Port Appin, Argyll

© Michael Starforth

Designed by D. G. Wallace

Printed by Nevisprint Ltd

ISBN 0 9530743 0 7

Acknowledgements and Preface

May I thank most warmly Lady Stewart of Appin, Mother of the present Chief of Clan Stewart of Appin, for her original suggestion that I should write this short history, based on the notes that I prepared for seven lectures given in Appin in 1996.

I should like to express deep gratitude to Dr Iain McNicol for generously spending so much time and trouble in looking after all the arrangements for the publication of the book. My special thanks are due to Mrs Mairi Smith, Chairperson of the Appin Historical Society, for all the support which she and members of the Society gave.

My utmost thanks are due to Stuart and Yvonne Carmichael, who most effectively advised throughout the project. Yvonne also coped with all the typing, managing to make sense of my none-too-clear handwriting.

May I add a note of warm gratitude to Mr Kenneth MacColl of Oban who most kindly lent to me a wide range of the Journals of the MacColl Society of the 1930s and 1940s, from which I have quoted in the text.

Appin Historical Society and I are all very grateful to Appin Community Co-operative for generously underwriting the publishing costs of the book, which has led to an earlier publication date.

On several occasions, I have used "The Stewarts of Appin" by John H.J. Stewart and Lt. Col. Duncan Stewart, published in 1880. This is an invaluable source of information. However, research in the present century has often gone beyond what was known in 1880 and occasionally I have been obliged to differ from this monumental work.

If I have devoted too much time and space to the Rising of 1745-46, the fault is entirely mine, but this was the last great effort by Clan Stewart of Appin and the other adherents of the Royal House of Stewart and came nearer to success than we are often led to believe. It led dramatically to the military and political end of the Clan System.

All author's royalties have been waived in favour of the
Appin Historical Society

Contents

The Origins of
Clan Stewart Of Appin

CHAPTER 1

The celebrated and gallant Clan Stewart of Appin has been, since the late 15th Century, a clan in its own right, but it is also the West Highland branch of the Royal House of Stewart. If we take the Clan`s Appin birth as 1463, it is not an ancient clan in the sense of MacDougall or Ross being ancient, but its Stewart ancestry, before the settlement in Lorn or in Appin, takes it back, it is believed, to the Celtic Breton Counts of Dol and, through them, to a noble house of Cornwall and Devon (Dumnonia) in the 6th Century.

Flaald or Fladald of Dol, son of the Chamberlain of the great Breton fortress-city and grandson of a Count of Dol, came first to England, then to Scotland, soon after William of Normandy`s conquest of the Saxon Kingdom and he may have accompanied the Saxon Princess Margaret to Scotland, where she married King Malcolm III. Flaald`s son, Alan Fitzflaald, returned to England in the suite of Princess Matilda of Scotland, who married Henry I in 1100. In 1102, Alan Fitzflaald, a man of distinguished ability, was made sheriff of Shropshire. He married Adelina de Hesding and his elder son became the progenitor of the Fitzalans, later Earls of Arundel and Dukes of Norfolk. The younger son, Walter Fitzalan Fitzflaald, joined the young David, Earl of Huntingdon, heir to the Scottish Throne. When the prince became King David I of Scots, he took Walter back with him to Scotland and, before 1141, created him High Steward of Scotland. David`s grandson, King Malcolm IV made the High Stewardship of Scotland hereditary for the heirs of Walter Fitzalan Fitzflaald in 1157 or 1161.

Walter of Dundonald, third High Steward of Scotland, took "Stewart" as the family surname about 1230. His son, Alexander, 4th High Steward, had two grandsons of particular interest to us.

Walter Stewart, 6th High Steward of Scotland, married the Lady Marjorie Bruce, elder daughter of King Robert the Bruce, and their son became the first Stewart King, on the death, without children, of Robert the Bruce`s only son, David II of Scots.

The second grandson of particular interest to us was Sir James Stewart of Perston, fourth son of John Stewart of Bonkyl (killed at Falkirk in 1298). James Stewart of Perston was the grandfather of the first Stewart Lord of Lorn, from whom the Stewarts of Appin descended. A genealogical table, (see Appendix I page 80) shows the descent of the first Stewart of Appin Chief from Flaald of Dol.*

Until the Wars of Independence, 1296 - 1328, the MacDougall descendants of Somerled the Great, had ruled all Argyll except Kintyre and Islay, under the distant suzerainty of the Kings of Scots. In 1306, the murder of the Red Comyn had caused his uncle, Alexander of Argyll, and his cousin and close friend, John MacDougall of Lorn, to change sides. In 1308, they forfeited their lands, but, at the end of the war, John of Lorn`s grandson, Ewan MacDougall, received back mainland Lorn,

* Holinshed, followed by George Buchanan in his 1570`s History of Scotland, claimed that Flaald was really "Fleance", sole surviving son of Banquo of Lochaber, murdered by Macbeth. Most modern historians feel that Flaald of Dol`s background is too well identified for this to be true.

from Kilmartin to LochLeven, but only Kerrera and Lismore from the great MacDougall island possessions. The remainder went to the MacDonalds of Islay, soon to be Lords of the Isles.

The restored Ewan of Lorn married Joan MacIsaac, grand-daughter of Robert the Bruce, through King Robert`s younger daughter, the Lady Matilda. As their respective grandfathers were mortal enemies, this may indeed have been a love-match. They had two daughters, but no sons. In the West Highlands in the 14th Century, it was not yet considered possible for a daughter to inherit the Chiefship of a Clan, while, by feudal law, daughters were co-heiresses.

Ewan of Lorn reconciled himself to the chiefship of his Clan passing to his cousin, Iain MacDougall, but he was anxious that mainland Lorn should not be divided. He consulted his wife`s uncle, King David II. The King produced two handsome young Stewart kinsmen, Sir John Stewart of Innermeath and Durrisdeer and his brother, Sir Robert, great-great-grandsons of the 4th High Steward. Sir John married Isabella, the younger of the co-heiresses and Sir Robert married Janet, her elder sister. Robert and Janet gave up any claim to half of Lorn, in exchange for Durrisdeer. Sir John Stewart, on the death of Ewan MacDougall, became first Stewart Lorn of Lorn, jure uxoris. Dunstaffnage Castle was his "capital", while Dunollie Castle was leased, for the time being, to Iain MacDougall of MacDougall.

The second Stewart Lord of Lorn was Robert, son of John and Isabella. He married the Lady Margaret Stewart, daughter of the Duke of Albany, who brought Royal Stewart blood to the Stewarts of Lorn, as Isabella MacDougall had brought Royal Bruce blood.

Their family had five sons and two daughters. The eldest son was John, third Stewart Lord of Lorn, and his younger brothers were, in order of age, Walter, Alan, David and Robert. One of the daughters married Alan, 10th Chief of Clan MacDougall.

It is not certain whom Sir John Stewart of Lorn married as his first wife, but two different traditions state that she was a daughter of the Lord of the Isles. They had three daughters, but no son and it was, above all, a son whom John Stewart longed to have, to whom to leave an intact inheritance of Lorn.

In 1445, the Lord of Lorn, returning to Dunstaffnage from a great cattle tryst at Crieff, met a Wedding Party in Glen Fillan. Well known throughout the Highlands and a sociable man of great charm, Sir John was cordially invited to the Wedding and enthusiastically accepted. He rode with the convivial party to Ardveich and there, in a fateful hour for Appin, he instantly fell in love with MacLaren of Ardveich`s daughter. His love was returned and Lorn explained the complexity of his position to Ardveich and his daughter. He stayed for several days and then regularly returned as often as he could.

Their son was born in 1446 and was christened Dugald. He, Dugald Stewart, was to become the de jure Lord of Lorn, but the actual first Chief of Clan Stewart of Appin. It was agreed that he should be brought up at Ardveich.

Three years later, in 1449, the lord of Lorn gave, as a marriage portion to his eldest daughter, Margaret, two small estates in Lorn (5 and a half merklands at Ardchattan and 7 pennylands at the head of Loch Awe) and a very generous proportion of his lands in Clackmannanshire and Perthshire. Soon afterwards, Isabel, the second daughter married Colin, Lord Campbell, Chief of Clan Campbell, and Marion, the youngest, married Arthur Campbell of Otter. As Margaret had married Colin Campbell of Glenurchy, the assumption seems to have been that the Campbells - and probably, by arrangement, Colin, Lord Campbell - would acquire the Lordship of Lorn, but the marriage portions of the two younger daughters contained no Lorn territory whatsoever. They consisted of large remaining estates in Perthshire, Clackmannanshire and Fife.

John Stewart of Lorn now had a son, albeit still not yet legitimate, and he was determined that Dugald should succeed to an undivided Lorn. His MacDonald wife was middle-aged and in poor health. It would be many years before Dugald would be old enough to succeed and, by that time, he might be legitimate. In 15th Century Scotland, unlike 15th Century England, a child was legitimised by a subsequent marriage of the parents.

In 1451, as a first step, John Stewart of Lorn formally granted to his nephew, John MacAlan MacDougall, Chief of Clan MacDougall, a most generous portion of Lorn, covering 127 merklands of Kerrera and of the mainland south and east of Dunollie Castle, which the MacDougall Chief had hitherto rented. The grant was partly to give his nephew the proper resources for a clan chief, but was also to reinforce a singular clause of the charter. In this, the MacDougall Chief was given some legal powers of guardianship over Lorn`s heir male ("alumnian et nutrimentum"). As Lorn`s brothers were in or approaching middle-age, this could have been intended to apply only to Dugald, still only 5 in 1451.

The following year, the Lord of Lorn took a dramatic step, emphasising that Lorn was NOT to be allowed to pass to the Campbells through his daughters. In June, 1451, he temporarily but formally surrendered the lands of Lorn to King James II and was immediately granted Lorn back, with fresh charters, entailing the lands and the Lordship to John Stewart`s heirs male. These were ostensibly his brothers and, successively, their heirs male, but, as the King must have known, the future heir male was intended to be Dugald Stewart.

In the late 1450s, the Lady of Lorn died, but it was at least five years before John Stewart of Lorn married Dugald`s mother. We do not know why the Lord of Lorn waited so long, instead of waiting only one year for the sake of decency, but the reason may lie in the behaviour of his brother-in-law, the Lord of the Isles.

By 1459, John, Lord of the Isles and Earl of Ross, was intriguing with the King of England and with the Earl of Douglas, exiled in England, against James II. By 1461, these intrigues had led to an infamous agreement to partition Scotland and to make its three different principalities subject to the English Crown. On 14th October 1461, the

Lord of the Isles and the Earl of Douglas had sealed their agreement to this in the Treaty of Ardtornish, which was countersigned by King Edward IV at Westminster in February 1462.

The agent of the plotters in Argyll was an able, but totally unscrupulous character, Alan MacCoul, an illegitimate grandson of an earlier MacDougall Chief. On behalf of the Lord of the Isles and the Earl of Douglas, Alan MacCoul approached John MacAlan MacDougall of MacDougall to join the conspiracy, as MacLean of Duart had already done. The MacDougall Chief indignantly refused, whereupon Alan MacCoul, who seems to have had a magnetic personality, raised a band of rebel MacDougalls and of Islesmen, seized Kerrera, kidnapped his own MacDougall Chief and imprisoned him in a small fort on Kerrera, to be starved to death. Ironically, the Chief was rescued by Colin, Lord Campbell, who was himself to use Alan MacCoul against Dugald Stewart in later years.

John Stewart of Lorn must have heard of the Ardtornish conspiracy from his MacDougall nephew. As his own brother-in-law, the Lord of the Isles, was the principal Scottish plotter and likely to invade Argyll at any time, Lorn, utterly loyal to the Crown, must have decided to wait for a more peaceful moment to bring his MacLaren love and his young son to Dunstaffnage for the wedding.

By spring, 1463, the Ardtornish revolt had burned itself nearly out, John of the Isles had attacked from Moray and Inverness to Arran and Bute, but had destroyed and not occupied. The English invasion had failed, but had cost Scotland dear, because James II had been killed by one of his own cannons at the siege of Roxburgh, leaving a young minor as King yet again.

Nevertheless, John Stewart of Lorn believed that the time had come and sent a strong escort to Balquhidder to bring his MacLaren bride and their son, now seventeen, to Dunstaffnage for the wedding, an event, which was well known throughout Argyll.

Ducan Stewart and his mother set out joyfully from Balquhidder for the ceremony at Dunstaffnage. Ardveich matched the Stewart escort with a troop of young MacLarens "men tall and sprightly and full of activity", as a MacLaren bard wrote. Four verses of his poem survived and were translated into English by a later Stewart. The first verse ran:

> *"The day you left Lochearnside,*
> *with your gentle mother on your arm,*
> *you were a hero, tall and powerful,*
> *and well did your mountain dress adorn you".**

* "The Stewarts of Appin", by John H.J. Stewart and Lt. Col. Dugald Stewart (1880).

The bard was not indulging in sentimental flattery. That Ducan Stewart was tall, powerful and heroic was shown repeatedly over the next few years, but, in 1463, he was still only seventeen and had no experience of legal or large scale political affairs.

The renegade Alan MacCoul, meanwhile, had laid a deadly plot. He was still being paid by the Lord of the Isles to weaken the defences of

Argyll and to undermine and to remove the royalist Lord of Lorn. Either at this time or within a month, however, he was also being subsidised by the Campbells and probably by Colin, Lord Campbell, now created Earl of Argyll.

The Ardveich party had been rapturously welcomed at Dunstaffnage and the wedding ceremony had been arranged for the following morning, in the Castle Chapel, 180 yards from the main doors of the great fortress. As Dunstaffnage had been completely at peace since 1308, no one had troubled with the fact that the last hundred yards to the Chapel lay through the edge of a wood. During the night, Alan MacCoul landed with a strongly armed force of rebel MacDougalls and Islesmen and concealed them in a skilful ambush on both sides of the path to the Chapel. The next morning, a gaily attired, but lightly armed procession, led by the Lord of Lorn, left the Castle to walk to the Chapel. There were Stewarts, MacLarens, loyal MacDougalls, MacNaughtons and other adherents of the Stewarts of Lorn. When the head of the procession had almost reached the Chapel, Alan MacCoul sprang his ambush. The wedding guests were numerous, but they had no armour and only their swords. The heavily armed attackers killed or wounded many of the guests, but MacCoul and a group of picked men concentrated on John Stewart, Lord of Lorn. His bodyguard was slain and he was stabbed and run through again and again. He fell, apparently dead. The MacLarens had been defending Dugald and his mother and Dugald, in his first serious fight, had been showing his great skill as a swordsman. In passionate fury and sorrow at seeing his father dead, Dugald would have pursued the murderers, who were withdrawing to seize the almost empty castle. The priest however, called him back, for the Lord of Lorn, though dying, was not yet dead. He was carried into the Chapel and there the priest, in front of Stewarts, loyal MacDougalls and MacLarens, married the just conscious Lord of Lorn to the woman whom he had loved so dearly for eighteen years. He was given the Last Rites and then he died. The able, influential, powerful John Stewart of Lorn was dead, but his long standing wish had been fulfilled: his beloved son, Dugald Stewart, was legitimised and was, by right, the fourth Stewart Lord of Lorn.

Alan MacCoul`s men now held Dunstaffnage Castle, impregnable to a force without artillery. No one among the bridal party knew what reserves the rebel MacCoul might have nor how many more Islesmen might arrive nor whether or not the Campbells, conspicuously absent from their Father-in-law`s wedding, might join with the Lord of the Isles` men. The Stewarts in Lorn were still small in numbers and, although the MacDougall Chief was loyal to the 1451 charter and agreement, his clan was split by the MacCoul revolt. Dugald decided that he must bring up the whole of his mother`s clan to regain Lorn.

He ordered his father`s lieutenants to raise all adherents loyal to the Stewart cause throughout Lorn and to meet him near Dalmally, when he returned with the MacLaren clansmen. That same afternoon, he started back for Ardveich with his heart-broken mother.

Dunstaffnage Chapel

11

It had been a day of terrible tragedy, but, on the same, day was born the remarkable and unique, three centuries old military alliance between the widely separate Clan MacLaren and Clan Stewart of Appin that finally blossomed on the field of Culloden.

Colin Campbell, Lord Argyll, and Campbell of Glenurchy may have absented themselves from the wedding, but they had kept themselves fully informed of events. They did not wish to use Campbell military force, if that could be avoided, so they sent urgent messages to their close kinsman, Duncan MacFarlane, 6th Chief of Clan MacFarlane, to bring his whole fighting force up to Dalmally. Duncan MacFarlane, from Western Loch Lomondside, knew little of the politics of Argyll, but he was a firm friend of the Campbells and he had his own reasons for disliking the Stewarts. His father had been heir male to the old Celtic Earldom of Lennox, but the Earldom had been given to the Stewart of Darnley (closely related to the Stewarts of Lorn) husband of the daughter of the last Celtic Earl. He raised his whole clan and marched, via Arrochar, Cairndubh and Inveraray towards Dalmally. Alan MacCoul, warned by Colin Campbell, left Dunstaffnage and moved to meet the MacFarlanes.

Dugald Stewart, meanwhile, had been given almost all the fighting men of Clan MacLaren and was forced marching back, through Glen Dochart and Strathfillan. The Stewart adherents of Lorn had come eastwards, some by Glencoe, but most by way of Loch Etive, and the latter force were able to tell Dugald Stewart, who met them beneath Ben Doran, that Alan MacCoul had left Dunstaffnage and was now encamped near Dalmally.

They knew nothing, however, of the MacFarlanes. Dugald and his lieutenants were puzzled at MacCoul`s recklessness, but decided to attack him at Dalmally the next morning. As the Campbells did not seem to be involved, they should outnumber him by at least two-to-one. They camped for the night at Leac-a-dotha, at the foot of Ben Doran.

Alan MacCoul had been joined that evening by the MacFarlanes. He and Duncan MacFarlane, informed by rebel MacDougall scouts of the whereabouts of the Stewarts and MacLarens, decided not to wait at Dalmally, but to make a surprise attack. Early the next morning they marched north east and threw themselves on Dugald Stewart`s hastily assembled army. We do not know the exact numbers involved but Dugald probably had about 700 men and MacCoul and MacFarlane about 800, including some Islesmen.

* "The Stewarts of Appin" (1880), Page 84

Beinn Doran

The battle of Leac-a-dotha was fierce and bloody, with heavy losses on both sides. The attackers, with some advantage in numbers, eventually forced the Stewarts and MacLarens back and, against his own inclinations, Dugald took the advice of his MacLaren and Stewart kinsmen and began to retreat northwards in relatively good order. He had lost almost half his Stewart and MacLaren fighting force. The MacFarlanes and Alan MacCoul`s men had suffered equally heavy losses, including the MacFarlane Chief, and were in no position to follow up their narrow victory in pursuit. The Stewarts and MacLarens withdrew, around the head of Loch Etive, into Appin and prepared to defend that district of Lorn against all comers.*

Meanwhile, in Edinburgh, John Stewart of Lorn`s next younger brother, Walter Stewart, supported by the Earl of Argyll, reported John Stewart`s murder to the Privy Council, stated that no marriage had taken place and that he, Walter Stewart, was now Lord of Lorn. Assured by Argyll, their most influential member, and by the dead man`s own brother, the Privy Council accepted the story and reported it to the powerless young boy who was King James III and to the Estates.

The following year, 1464, the Estates somewhat belatedly ordered royal troops to Dunstaffnage to retake the Castle and to punish MacCoul, "the punicion of Alan MacCoul, guhilk as cruelyn slayin John Lord Lorn the King`s cusing" (cousin). The royal troops never appear to have reached Dunstaffnage and Alan MacCoul remained there as long as it suited Colin Campbell of Argyll. No step was taken by any Campbell to avenge the murder of the father-in-law of three distinguished Campbells. Neither did the dead man`s brother lift a finger against the assassins. On the contrary, Walter Stewart supplied Alan MacCoul with money and mercenaries to continue his war with Walter`s "illegitimate nephew".

Significantly, Walter Stewart may have called himself Lord of Lorn in Edinburgh, but he made no written submission towards recognition and he was careful to go nowhere near Lorn, where he was detested. Whatever people in far off Edinburgh thought, the truth was known throughout Argyll, though it was not until 1885, in his "Records of Argyll", that Lord Archibald Campbell, younger brother of the 9th Duke of Argyll, conceded that John Stewart of Lorn`s marriage had taken place and that Dugald Stewart was legitimate. The Stewart adherents of Dugald`s father throughout Lorn voted with their feet. There were not very many of them but, rather than submit to Walter Stewart or to Colin Campbell, they moved to Appin in the "Anveich Mor" and joined Dugald Stewart, when Walter`s behaviour in Edinburgh became known. It is a measure of the indignation and revulsion felt towards Walter Stewart that, despite Walter being a popular name in the House of Stewart, no Chief of Clan Stewart of Appin and no Chieftain of any of its branches ever gave the name Walter to a son.

In Appin and Lismore, the local families who had been adherents, first of the MacDougalls, then of the Stewart Lords of Lorn, unanimously accepted Dugald as their Chief. The principal families were the MacLays (later anglicised as Livingstones), the MacGillemichaels (anglicised as Carmichaels) and the MacColls.

They were families rather than small clans; they were accustomed to being tenants of the Lords of Lorn; and, with their tenancies willingly renewed, they enthusiastically accepted the young and energetic Dugald Stewart. From 1463, Clan Stewart of Appin was effectively in being. It needed a battle and hopefully a victory to weld it into a conscious clan.

For the next few years, Dugald Stewart consolidated Appin and Lismore, fortified the small hunting lodge which was to become Castle Stalcaire, and studied military and legal affairs. Each year, he reminded his enemies of his claim to Lorn and trained his clansmen by damaging

Dunstaffnage Castle

13

raids on southern Lorn, below Loch Creran, which was now firmly in Campbell hands.

At last, in 1468, Colin Campbell of Argyll and Walter Stewart decided on a major offensive to destroy the de jure Lord of Lorn. Alan MacCoul, their most able agent in Lorn, was entrusted with large funds and with numerous mercenaries and was told to invade Appin. He still had some rebel MacDougalls (but _Not_ Clan MacDougall) and he is said to have been reinforced by many MacFarlanes. With an army larger than any force that Dugald Stewart could raise, MacCoul crossed the Creran and struck north. He was followed, but not joined, by a considerable body of Campbells, who occupied the northern side of the River Creran and Loch Creran, but took no further part.

Dugald Stewart, who had received advance warning from friendly MacDougalls, had sent the news on to the MacLarens. As both Clans were always to do, they responded well and the flower of Clan MacLaren marched swiftly to Appin. Dugald Stewart gathered his forces at what is now Portnacroish, but, as the invaders approached, he deployed his men, Stewarts and MacLarens, MacLays and MacGillemichaels, MacColls and Combichs, along the ridge above the present Episcopalian Church.

Alan MacCoul`s men, who had expected to find them in front of Castle Stalcaire, now found their enemy obliging them to fight at right angles to their line of advance/retreat and to fight with their backs to the water. The invaders had an advantage in numbers, but Dugald Stewart had the advantage of ground. Before the invaders could fully dress their column into line, he gave the order for a down hill charge.

The Battle of Stalc was fiercely fought. The mercenaries, Highland and Lowland, were tough and experienced and the MacFarlanes and rebel MacDougalls were literally fighting for their lives, but the élan of Dugald Stewart`s troops was irresistible. The end came when Alan MacCoul was struck dead by Dugald Stewart himself in the centre. John Stewart of Lorn had been avenged. The remainder of the invading force retreated, fighting stubbornly to the shore, where they died almost to a man. Only a few of their right wing escaped down the Strath of Appin to bring the news to their Campbell allies.

News of the defeat caused Walter Stewart to decide that continued struggle was pointless. He offered the Lordship of Lorn to Argyll. This was what Colin Campbell had intended all along, but he was sensible enough to see that he would have to accept a Lorn without Appin. The two sent emissaries with a compromise to Dugald Stewart. He could keep Appin - to be held direct from the Crown - but he must not attempt to take more of Lorn or else he must face war with the whole of Clan Campbell and its allies. Heartened by Stalc, Dugald, still only 22, would like to have fought on, but his small forces could not hope to resist the largest Clan of Argyll with its allied clans.

In the autumn of 1469, Dugald Stewart, rightful Lord of Lorn, now Chief of Appin, reluctantly ceded his rights to the remainder of Lorn to Walter, his uncle and also ceded Innermeath, which he had never seen.

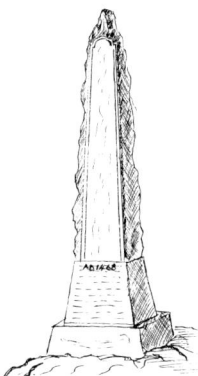

Memorial to the Battle of Stalc.

On 30th November, Walter Stewart came to an agreement with Argyll and on 28th March 1470, Walter took seisin of Lorn, which he had not dared to do before.

On 14th April, Walter resigned the title and lands of Lorn, less Appin, to King James III, still a minor. Three days later, on 17th April 1470, the young King granted the Lordship of Lorn to Argyll. Walter Stewart is said by many historians to have received Innermeath "in exchange", a ridiculous remark when one considers that Innermeath belonged either to Dugald or to Walter, but certainly not to Argyll. Walter became a Lord of Parliament as "Lord Innermeath".

Dugald Stewart, who, but for betrayal by his uncle and by his Campbell brothers-in-law, should have been Lord of Lorn, became first Chief of Clan Stewart of Appin. The Battle of Stalc had done more than free Appin from Campbell control. It had welded the Stewarts and their local adherents into a clan which to become one of the bravest and noblest in Scotland.

Early Clan Chiefs and some Branch Chieftains

Despite the recognition by the Earl of Argyll and by Glenorchy, in 1469, of Dugald Stewart`s right to hold the whole of Appin, including Lismore, from the Crown, Argyll`s clansmen continued to hold a narrow strip of Appin north of Invercreran and Loch Creran and to hold almost one third of Lismore. These illegally occupied lands Argyll "gave" to Glenorchy, but he warned Dugald Stewart that the full fighting force of the Campbells of Argyll would be behind Glenorchy`s men. The Stewarts of Appin were not yet strong enough to oust Glenorchy, but they demonstrated their refusal to accept the situation by raiding both Glenorchy`s own lands and the Argyll Campbell lands of Barcaldine. The two outstanding strips of Stewart of Appin territory were not handed over until after Dugald Stewart`s death, in 1497, but the last years of his life were made more pleasant by the friendship of the young King, James IV, who had succeeded his murdered father in 1488, when he was only sixteen. James IV had a passion for hunting and hawking and discovered that Appin was an excellent venue for both.

Dugald Stewart spent much of the first twenty years of his chiefship getting to know and becoming popular with the tenants who worked most of Appin. Surprise has sometimes been expressed that so small a number of Stewarts and their original retainers, who had come to Appin in 1463-64, had been accepted by the more numerous older inhabitants, who had their own "headmen". These earlier inhabitants, however, had not owned their lands and had not regarded themselves as separate "clans". Since 1388, they had been the tenants of the Stewart

Lords of Lorn at Dunstaffnage and, for 230 years before that, they had been the tenants of the MacDougall Lords of Lorn. They accepted Dugald as the rightful heir and they kept the tenancies that they had held. In the 15th Century, they were extended families of comparatively small numbers. Some Appin land was not yet occupied and this was distributed and developed by the lesser Stewart gentry.

The principal adherents among the earlier inhabitants were the Macleays or MacClays, whose name later became "Englished" to Livingston; the Macgillemichaels who were later better known as Carmichaels; and the MacColls who were originally MacDonalds, who had strayed across Loch Leven in the mid 14th Century. These are sometimes called Septs of the Stewarts of Appin, which is, in effect, what they were, but they were more correctly adherents.

There were indeed two Clans Stewart of Appin. Socially, Clan Stewart comprised those of the name of Stewart and many more with Stewart blood through intermarriage. More important was the military and political concept of Clan Stewart of Appin and this included the Macleays, the Carmichaels, the MacColls and other adherents. The MacLeays or Livingstons* were mainly settled on Lismore, while the Carmichaels were partly on Lismore and partly on the mainland, between Strath of Appin and Duror. The MacColls were found between Ardsheal and Ballachulish and south and east of the latter**.

Two smaller, but significant adherent groups were the Combichs and the MacInnes`s. The Combichs or MacCombichs seem to have been descended from a family with a nickname in North Appin. There were enough descendants for 5 to die and 3 to be wounded in the Appin Regiment at Culloden. The MacInnes families, originally from Morvern in the early 15th Century, were spread throughout Argyll and Lochaber, but those in Appin adhered closely to the Stewarts and 4 died at Culloden. The names of the non-Stewart fighting men who died or were wounded at Culloden were listed by the Regiment under family names. The total casualty list is reproduced as Appedix III on pages 84 and 85 but it is worth noting now that the largest group, the MacColls, lost 18 killed and 15 wounded.

*There is still a Livingstone of Bachuill on Lismore.

The McRobs, though commonly using that name, were a full sept of Clan Stewart. They were Stewart by blood, being descended from a natural son of Robert, son of Dugald, 1st of Appin. In the Regimental lists for Culloden, they appear under the Stewarts. Their tenancies were in Glenduror, Lettermore and Acharn.

** A note on the believed origins of the MacColls, drawn from the Journal of The MacColl Society, January 1948, appears on page 21.

Dugald Stewart of Appin married a daughter of his first cousin, John MacAlan MacDougall of MacDougall, the unfortunate chief against whom Alan MacCoul had rebelled. They had three sons, Duncan, Alan and Robert, of whom Duncan and Alan were to succeed as second and third Chiefs respectively. Dugald Stewart, still in his early fifties, died as he would have wished, fighting for his closest allies, his Mother`s clan, the MacLarens.

In 1497, he received a laconic message, conveying an appeal for help, from Balquhidder. A MacLaren raiding party had lifted a large herd of cattle from the MacDonalds of Keppoch and had brought them safely across Rannoch - the total number being six or seven times higher than was at all reasonable. Regarding this, not as a small creagh, but as an act of war, the whole Clan MacDonald of Keppoch was being mobilised to march on Balquhidder. The MacLarens, never more than a small clan, would be out numbered by four or five to one.

Dugald Stewart sent his swiftest runner off to the MacLarens, raised every man that he could in a few hours and then marched through Glencoe, with whose MacDonalds he was on terms of close friendship, and crossed the passes of the Black Mount. Moving very swiftly, the Appin force`s scouts overtook the large MacDonald column before it reached upper Glen Orchy. That evening, a MacLaren brought news that his clansmen would be at the head of Glen Orchy within an hour of dawn. Confident that surprise would make up for lack of numbers, Dugald decided on a sudden dawn attack.

Soon after dawn, he threw his Stewarts, MacColls, Carmichaels and other adherents against the breakfasting MacDonalds. Before the Keppoch MacDonalds could recover and use their weight of numbers the MacLarens reached the battlefield from the south-east. Although the Stewart-MacLaren allies combined had only half the MacDonald strength, they utterly defeated the latter, with very heavy losses, including the Chief`s brother. At the heart of the battle and with victory in his grasp, died Dugald Stewart of Appin.

He was succeeded by his eldest son, Duncan, who was Chief for only fifteen years, but who received the warm friendship of King James IV and many honours from him. It was for the King and possibly with financial help from the King that Duncan Stewart of Appin rebuilt Castle Stalcaire on Creag an Sgairbh (the Cormorants` Rock). That there had been a small fort on the islet is indicated by the fact that Dugald had chosen it as his first headquarters and had drawn up his small army just opposite the islet at the Battle of Stalc, 1468. The Royal Commission on Ancient and Historical Monuments suggests that Castle Stalcaire or Stalker was built by Alan, 3rd Chief, for James V about 1540. James IV, however was even more fond of Appin than James V and was frequently there, whether for hunting or en route to deal with rebellious Islesmen. Probably Castle Stalker was built partly by Duncan for James IV and further enlarged by his brother, Alan, for James V.

On 14th January 1500, a Royal Charter confirmed recognition of Duncan`s hereditary right to all Appin, including Lismore. The same Charter, while confirming the MacDonald occupation of Glencoe, transferred the rent for Glencoe to Duncan Stewart. Ballachulish was recognised as a part of Appin. Immediately afterwards, the King ordered Campbell of Glenorchy to give up his illicit possession of the southern strip of Appin and of a third of Lismore to their rightful owner, Duncan Stewart. On 24th September 1501, the Earl of Argyll and Duncan Campbell of Glenorchy formally recognised Duncan Stewart as holding, direct from the Crown, the whole of Appin and Lismore, by right of heritage from his deceased father, Dugald Stewart of Appin.

Castle Stalker

Shortly afterwards during a visit to the West Highlands to stamp out further unrest among the Islesmen (John, Lord of the Isles, had surrendered his powers and titles to the King in 1494, but the Islesmen were urging his half-brother, Donald of Sleat, to declare himself Lord of the Isles), James IV created Duncan King`s Chamberlain of the Isles.  For the Chief of a quite small clan, this was a great honour and demonstrated the King`s absolute faith in him. It also led indirectly to his murder twelve years later.

On 9th July 1512, Duncan Stewart of Appin received from the King by charter the life rent of Inverlochy and part of Mamore. This royal gift was the final provocation to a neighbouring clan chief. During the last rising of the Lord of the Isles and again while the Islesmen rose when their Lord was in the King`s power, one of their major allies was MacLean of Duart. The MacLeans had long been associated with successive Lords of the Isles and they felt that they owed little fealty to the Kings of Scots. Lachlan MacLean of Duart had unwillingly surrendered before the power of the King, but he resented someone he thought of as a half-lowland upstart being given authority over him as King`s Chamberlain of the Isles and his resentment became overwhelming when Duncan Stewart was given Lochaber territories which the Lord of the Isles had promised to him, Duart.

In truth, Duncan Stewart was a Highlander. His father had been brought up as a Gaelic speaking Highlander in Balquhidder and his mother was the daughter of a MacDougall chief. He could speak Lowland Scots, but his native tongue was Gaelic and it was as a Highland Chief, with Highland concepts of hospitality, that he received, late in 1512, an invitation to visit Lachlan MacLean at Duart. Not realising the ferocious hatred felt for him by the MacLean chief, Duncan not only accepted the invitation but took with him to Mull only Sorley MacColl, his wet foot Gille.

The Stewart chief was entertained lavishly for three days, after which he declared that he must return to Castle Stalker. There are at least three different versions of what happened next (the most horrific being in the Records of Argyll), but all are agreed completely on the murder of Duncan Stewart of Appin and his henchman. The Stewart tradition - the most moderate - states that Duncan found Sorley MacColl being first taunted, then buffeted and finally attacked with swords and axes by seven or eight MacLeans. The Chief went to Sorley`s aid, but in vain.  The MacLean Chief then emerged and ordered Duncan`s murder. The Stewart fought well, but was overwhelmed and killed. His body was left lying on a rock between castle and shore. *

* Some traditions give 1519 as the date of the murder, but this is not possible in view of Alan`s leadership at Flodden and of his territorial dispositions immediately after the Flodden campaign.

Duart Castle

News of the murder reached Lismore before it reached Castle Stalker. The MacLeay of Bachuill, headman of the MacLeays of Lismore, took a boat across to Duart at dead of night, recovered his chief`s body and drove holes with his dirk in the bilge planks of the MacLean boats lying on the shore beneath the castle. In one account he is joined by his red-headed daughters; in another version by several kinsmen. As the MacLeays rowed away, they were seen by a castle sentry who raised the alarm. They were pursued (or slowed up deliberately to be pursued) by several boatloads of MacLeans, whose leaking boats gradually began to sink. Many of the MacLeans were drowned. The MacLeay of Bachuill buried Duncan Stewart, 2nd Chief of Appin, in the church of St Moluag.

Duncan Stewart had not married and was succeeded by his younger brother Alan, married to a Cameron of Lochiel, who became third Chief of the Clan. Only a few months after he became Chief, Alan had to muster the whole clan in answer to the summons of James IV, who was raising a large army to invade Northern England to release the pressure from Henry VIII on Scotland`s French allies. This was the splendid army which was so tragically destroyed at Flodden. Alan Stewart of Appin took his five sons as subordinate commanders to Flodden. All six fought well, according to contemporary sources, yet all six survived, when 10,000 Scottish nobles, knights and soldiers were killed, stubbornly standing their ground. The reason must be that, serving as they did on the right wing, under the Earls of Argyll and Lennox, the West Highlanders first broke Constable`s left wing brigade, but then, while they were totally disordered after a wild charge, were driven off the field altogether by Sir Edward Stanley`s brigade. They were not, therefore, part of the Scottish centre that stood and died until darkness intervened. Even then, the Stewarts were lucky. Before Stanley`s brigade was recalled from pressing the retreating clans, Argyll and Lennox had been among the thirteen Scottish Earls killed.

Soon after their return to Appin and perhaps to cheer his men, Alan Stewart divided much of his territory between his sons. Duncan, the eldest, was formally proclaimed his heir to Appin, Strathgarry was given to John, Achnacone to Dugald, Fasnacloich to James and Invernahyle to Alexander (see genealogical table Appendix II page82). Thus were founded the first branches of Clan Stewart of Appin.

The death of James IV at Flodden threw Scotland back into the weakened state of royal minority. The new Earl of Argyll took every advantage of his influential position in the Privy Council. Though Donald Dubh of the Isles was still a prisoner, the Islesmen rose again, under Donald MacDonald of Lochalsh. Argyll secured the appointment of commander of all the royal forces in the West Highlands against the Islesmen. He was powerful enough to force Alan Stewart to grant him a charter of Apprisement of Fasnacloich and Glasdrum. Then, in 1522, Argyll`s brother, Campbell of Calder received, by dubious means, from MacLaine of Lochbuie, the obsolete charter of Duror, Glencoe and parts of Lochiel, granted before the 1494 rising and then countermanded by James IV.

The Stewarts, the MacDonalds of Glencoe and the Camerons banded together in successful resistance to this. Eventually, by Argyll`s insistence, Campbell of Calder was recognised as overlord of Duror, part of Lochiel and Glencoe, provided that he did not interfere and provided that he remitted more than half the rent. In Appin, this unjust arrangement affected only Duror, but the events of the years 1520 to 1530 greatly reinforced the friendship between the Stewarts, the Camerons and the MacDonalds of Glencoe.

In 1530, Colin, Earl of Argyll died and was succeeded by Archibald, 4th Earl, who employed the same tactics for aggrandisement. A few years later, however, Argyll and Campbell of Calder were arrested for stirring up strife in the West Highlands for their own ends. Argyll was soon released, but the now adult James V never restored his offices. In 1538, having revoked the unjust charters of his minority, the King granted a fresh charter to his "much beloved kinsman", Alan Stewart of Appin, for the lands of Duror, described in great detail, to be held by Alan and his heirs and successors direct from the Crown.

Duncan Stewart, younger of Appin, is generally known as 4th Chief of Appin, but he did not infact outlive his father, Alan, who lived until 1562, when he may have been ninety. However, as Alan became elderly, he may have granted some chiefly powers to his heir. Duncan married Janet, daughter of the Earl of Huntly. He had one son, John, nicknamed the "Gordonich ban", as he had inherited fair hair from his mother. The date of Duncan Stewart`s death is unknown, though a tradition states that he was murdered by the MacDonalds of Keppoch. It is suggested that this must have been in or just before 1547, because Donald-nan-ord, 2nd of Invernahyle, and not Duncan Stewart, younger of Appin, led the Stewart of Appin contingent to the Battle of Pinkie in that year. Other traditions say that he was disabled in 1547 and was not murdered until the late 1550s.

At any rate, the aged Alan Stewart was succeeded, in 1562, by his grandson, John Gordonich Ban, 5th Chief of Appin. Like several other chiefs and lairds, John Stewart of Appin was partly, though not deeply, involved in a Campbell-Gordon conspiracy in 1592 to murder the Bonnie Earl of Moray and probably to murder also the young Earl of Argyll. The principal Campbell conspirator was Campbell of Lochnell, heir to the Earldom, if the young Argyll died. John Stewart of Appin had married Katherine of Lochnell and it was as Lochnell`s brother-in-law that Appin found himself on the fringes of the plot. The Gordon plotters murdered the Earl of Moray and their Campbell co-plotters murdered Campbell of Calder, senior administrator of the young Argyll`s estates. There was a revulsion of feeling, the remainder of the plot failed and a very angry young Argyll survived.

By his first wife, Katherine, John Stewart had a son, Duncan, who was to succeed him. After Katherine`s death, John married a daughter of MacDonald of Moidart and their son, John, became 1st of Ardsheal. Later, in the 18th Century, when the male chiefly line of Appin died out, the Ardsheal chieftains succeeded, as they were nearest in blood to the main male line. John Stewart, 5th of Appin died in 1595 and was succeeded by his son Duncan, who took the clan into the 17th Century, which was to be dominated by civil wars.

In a very short history like this, it is not possible to follow in detail the development of the branches and septs of the Stewarts of Appin. Even were it possible, accounts would be uneven, partly because some branches kept fuller records than others, but much more because most early papers of the Stewart branches were destroyed, when the houses of chieftains were burned either in the 1644-47 War or in the 1745-46 War.

However, individuals from the branches, particularly from Ardsheal and from Invernahyle, appear flamboyantly from time to time on the pages of History.

Firstly, one should look briefly at the non-Stewart adherents or "septs" of Appin, since their origins in Appin were considerably older. The MacLeays` (Livingstons) origin in Lismore is so old that we can only guess. They were on Lismore in the 1130-1200 days of Somerled the Great and of his eldest son, Dougal. They themselves believe that they were on Lismore when St. Moluag was on the island in the 6th Century. This may well be true, since the senior MacLeay was the MacLeay of Bachuill, hereditary Keeper of the Staff of St. Moluag. They were a quiet, tenacious people, small in numbers, always loyal to the Chief of Appin and still contributing fighting men in 1745-46.

The origins of the MacGillemichaels or McIlmichaels, later better known as Carmichaels, also go back into the mists of time before Somerled. It is known that Dougal had MacGillemichael tenants in Appin in the late 12th century, but it is likely that his great-grandfather, Gilla Andomnan of Argyll, had them as tenants also.

MacColl traditions state that their first ancestor in Appin, Black Solomon, son of Coll, son of "MacDonald of the Isles" (probably John, 1st Lord of the Isles), had a brother-in-law, MacGillemichael, and that both were given lands in about 1360 in the areas of Ballachulish and Duror. Together, they fought the MacDonalds of Glencoe, who had only arrived a generation earlier and who were descended from Iain Fraoch, the younger, natural brother of John, Lord of the Isles. If, however, this is meant to imply that the MacGillemichaels arrived in Appin only in about 1360, then it is incorrect. It is known from MacDougall sources that the MacGillemichaels had been tenants in Appin at least since the 1160s and probably much earlier. The Carmichaels, as they will be called for convenience, were also intensely loyal to the Stewart of Appin Chiefs, fought in all their wars up to and including Culloden, and sometimes intermarried with Stewart Chieftains` families.

As noted already, the MacColls, who were MacDonalds by ancestry, settled in northern Appin in the mid-14th Century, as tenants of Ewan, last MacDougall Lord of Lorn. They were enthusiastic fighting men and, after three generations of Stewart Lords, from 1388, they were happy to adhere to the Stewarts of Appin. By the 17th Century, they were providing more men for the Stewart of Appin contingents than any other non Stewart name.

To return to the Stewart branches, the most active in the 16th century appears to have been that of Invernahyle. Alexander, 1st of Invernahyle married Margaret MacDonald of Lochan, Moidart. They had a son Donald, who was to become the most famous Appin Stewart of the century. Alexander was out fishing alone on a small island near his home one morning, when a birlinn full of Campbells, commanded by the brother of Dunstaffnage, happened to draw near him. Oblivious to all but the fish, he was surprised and killed after a short struggle. The islet is said, by tradition, to have been adjacent to Eilean Stalcaire, but this makes little sense of what followed. Seeing approaching Campbells, the

Moidart nurse of baby Donald seized him, fled from the back of the house to the woods and made her way north. Even if Castle Stalcaire was not completely built by 1515 or 1516, whatever fortress was there would surely have had some garrison. It is possible that the incident happened at the mouth of Loch Creran, near Invernahyle's half-built and perhaps unmanned new house.

The Moidart nurse, determined to trust no one, took the child back to her own family in Lochan, where her father was blacksmith and a brilliant swordsmith. There the boy grew up, strong, tall and an excellent swordsman. As he could also forge a good blade himself, he was known as Domhnull-nan-Ord or Donald of the Hammers. When he returned to Appin, at 17 or 18, he was immediately recognised by his grandfather, Alan Stewart of Appin, and installed as Donald, 2nd of Invernahyle.

He did not wait long before taking a picked raiding party down Loch Linnhe to Dunstaffnage, where he launched a ferocious attack, killing many Campbells, including the chieftain's brother, who had killed his own father. His father and his honour avenged, he skilfully extricated his men and sailed back to Invernahyle with light losses. This was the man, who was invited, much later, to command the Stewart of Appin force which took part in the Pinkie campaign of 1547.

It is worth noting that his elder son, Duncan, was so opposed to the unnecessary use of force, while nevertheless having ample courage, that he was respectfully known as Duncan the Peaceful. To the fury of his formidable father, Duncan later fell in love with and insisted on marrying Helen Campbell of Dunstaffnage, great niece of his grandfather's murderer. Donald of the Hammers eventually forgave his heir and welcomed Helen. When his father died, at about 77, in 1590, Duncan became 3rd of Invernahyle.

In 1547, when the Appin force returned from Pinkie, Donald of the Hammers persuaded the now elderly Appin that, although the Camerons to the north and the MacDonalds to the east were friendly, a strong Stewart outpost should be established to guard the narrows of Loch Leven and the entry along its southern shore. To this Appin agreed and gave the lands of Ballachulish and the duty of defending this important area to Allan Stewart, third son of Donald of the Hammers, who had particularly distinguished himself early in the Battle of Pinkie, when Angus's vanguard repulsed the English heavy cavalry. (That Pinkie became a disgraceful Scottish defeat was largely due to the incompetence of the Scottish Commander-in-Chief, the Earl of Arran). Thus was founded, 1547, the fresh Stewart House of Ballachulish. Most of its tenants were to be Stewart McRobs (Sliochd Ailein'ic Rob) and McColls.

As has been noted, Duncan, 6th of Appin, had a younger half-brother, John, the son of John Gordonich Bann's second wife, Mary MacDonald of Keppoch. In the 1590s, this John was given Ardsheal and founded the senior cadet branch of the Stewarts of Appin, but that is a matter for the 17th Century and the next chapter.

Appin in the
17th Century Civil Wars

Chapter 3

For the West Highlands, the opening two or three decades of the 17th Century were comparatively peaceful. In 1603, James VI of Scots succeeded Queen Elizabeth to the Crown of England and thereafter, in his own partly true words "governed Scotland with his pen". The Earl of Argyll, as usual, stirred up discord and then seized the lands of those appearing to rebel. However, in 1615, his debts in the Lowlands forced him to flee; he began to intrigue with Scottish and Irish Catholic nobles in Spain; and then, to the horror of his pious Presbyterian heir, Archibald, Lord Lorn, he became a Roman Catholic, denounced King James VI and I and entered the King of Spain`s service. This gave a blessed degree of peace to Appin and indeed to most of Argyll. Lorn was allowed by the King to inherit the estates and to act as chief of Clan Campbell, but he had to walk warily , lest his father`s treason caused the estates to be confiscated to the Crown. Not until 1636 was Appin to suffer anything from the Chief of Clan Campbell and then it was a claim by Lorn to the estate of Glasdrum in Glencreran. Lorn won the case, but was careful to reinstate immediately the tenancies of the three MacColls, who had received sasines for these farms from Duncan Stewart, 7th of Appin, in 1617, confirmed in 1623.* After this typically legalistic act, Lorn became too busy in Edinburgh with events leading up to the National Covenant and the so called Bishops` Wars to give much thought to Appin.

The best known act of Duncan, 7th of Appin, meanwhile, had been to lose Castle Stalker by his own folly. On a night of heavy drinking and conviviality with his neighbour, Campbell of Airds, Duncan Stewart, who must have been drunk almost beyond thought, pledged Airds to give him Castle Stalker in exchange for an eight-oared birlinn. In the morning, when the enormity of what he had done had sunk in, Appin begged Airds to rescind the agreement.

When Airds refused, Appin felt that his honour obliged him to keep his promise and Castle Stalker was granted to Campbell of Airds. The chieftains and clansmen were furious, but could not stand in the way of their Chief`s honour. All they could do was to announce formally that the Clan now regarded, as their "leader in war", Appin`s brother John, until such a time as the Chief``s son was old enough. Fortunately, when next war came, in the 1640s, the son, whose mother was the daughter of Lochiel, had been Chief for some years. This was Duncan Mor Stewart, 8th of Appin, a good fighting man and a dedicated royalist.

The causes of the Civil Wars that were to engulf England, Scotland and Ireland in the mid-17th Century are far beyond the scope of this short book. Nevertheless, it is important, in order to understand the attitudes of the Stewarts of Appin, to realise that the major causes differed as between the three Kingdoms. In England, the two principal causes were the King`s refusal to hand over power over the tiny regular army and

* Journal of the MacColl Society, January 1937.

Birlinn

the militia to the two-thirds of the House of Commons and little more than one-third of the House of Lords, who eventually opposed him in war (at least one hundred M.P.s joined the King`s side). Equally important to the King was his refusal to reform the Church of England.

In Scotland, however, military power lay in the hands of the great Lowland landowners and Highland chiefs. There, the chief cause of war was the King`s refusal to sign the Covenant and allow the Presbyterian Church to have a monopoly of theocratic power in Scotland. The majority of Lowlanders were Presbyterian, except in Aberdeen and the North-East. Most of the major Clans, however, except the Campbells, were Episcopalian, while a few had remained Roman Catholic. The Stewarts of Appin and their allies, the Camerons, most MacDonalds and the MacLeans were Episcopalian and therefore tended to support the King, but they remained quiet at first, because they were completely cut off from the King`s English supporters and because Argyll, by far the most influential layman in Covenanting circles and rapidly gaining power every month, already viewed them with deep suspicion.

In Ireland, one can only briefly mention that, in 1641, the heavy but just hand of Strafford having been withdrawn, the majority of Irish, still Roman Catholic, with most of their lands confiscated and with few civil rights, rose in rebellion against their English, Scottish and occasionally Irish Protestant Landlords. The Anglo-Scottish-Irish Protestant camp was itself divided between the King`s supporters, under the Earl of Ormonde, who were willing to give some concessions to the Irish, and the Scottish Covenanters and English Parliamentary adherents, who would come to no compromise agreement at all.

The main Scottish Covenant Army was, in 1644, sent to England to help Parliament against the King, partly on the somewhat spurious promise that England would become Presbyterian. Another division of the Covenant Army was in Ulster, helping the Protestant settlers to re-establish their dominance.

Then two events occurred which transformed the situation in Scotland. In July 1644, there landed in the West of Scotland a small, but veteran force of about 1,200 Ulster Catholic troops, under the command of Alistair McColl Keitach (Colkitto, in popular parlance, though Colkitto was the nickname of his father). Since the Catholic Irish, were, rightly or wrongly, feared and hated throughout Protestant Scotland, Argyll was correct in thinking that this venture, by itself, in August 1644, was likely to come to nothing. The second event, however, was the arrival in the Central Highlands, of the Marquis of Montrose, who was to prove himself a master of regular warfare and the most brilliant guerrilla leader of the century. He had crossed the Border and the Lowlands, disguised as groom to his two friends. Hearing in Perthshire that the Irish were approaching Blair Atholl from the west, while the Stewarts and Robertsons of Atholl were mustering, on the orders of the Privy Council, to fight them, Montrose hastened to Blair and was just in time to prevent a conflict. Both sides at once recognised his King`s Commission as Commanding General in Scotland and he marched on

Perth at the head of 2,000 men, to be joined by royalists, mainly his own Grahams, on the way. He easily won his first victory at Tibbermuir.

Rumours of Montrose`s early victories reached Appin along with suggestions that the Stewarts, Camerons and MacLeans should do no more than hold Northern Argyll and Lochaber for the Crown and threaten Argyll`s northern flank, for the time being. As most of the "Irish" were MacDonalds of Antrim and descendants of the MacDonalds of Islay, driven out two generations earlier by the Campbells, the MacDonalds of Glengarry and Clanranald did join them in some numbers. Then came Montrose`s extraordinary march on Inveraray, Argyll`s own capital burgh, which took Argyll and the Covenanters completely by surprise. Argyll, at Inveraray himself, as Montrose`s force marched down the allegedly impenetrable Glen Aray, fled in his galley. He desperately needed regular Lowland troops, experienced Campbell regiments from Ulster and ships. He also believed, not without reason, that his death would mean the end of the Covenanting government. Some of his clansmen held out in the old Inveraray Castle, for whose walls Montrose had no artillery, and the rest fled to the hills. Fortunately for both sides the winter, so far, was remarkably mild.

Once the heart of Campbell country had been ravaged, Montrose had to withdraw his men to the safety of the Central Highlands. The invasion had been brilliantly successful. Argyll`s once all powerful reputation had been damaged; the MacDonalds, Ulster and Scottish, had avenged at least some of the many wrongs suffered at Campbell hands; and the King had been aided by the withdrawal of some Scottish regiments from England. All would be lost, however, if Montrose and his army were trapped in Argyll.

Sending messengers ahead to call out the reliably royalist Stewarts of Appin and Camerons, Montrose marched north up Loch Awe and through the Pass of Brander. At Connell, only one large and three small boats could be found to cross Loch Etive, but the army was ferried across in twenty-four hours of continuous crossing and re-crossing. The Campbell garrison at Dunstaffnage did nothing; neither, next day, did the garrison of Barcaldine.

In friendly Appin, Montrose heard reliable news of the enemy. General William Baillie, with a large force of Lowland Covenanters and regular troops from England, was at Perth, ready to march north or west. The Earl of Seaforth, with the northern Covenanters, 5,000 strong, was waiting at Inverness. Argyll, with a stroke of imagination, which was probably inspired by the best of the Campbell commanders, Duncan Campbell of Auchinbreck, whom he had recalled from Ulster, landed at Inverlochy, with 2,000 Campbells (many of them experienced soldiers from Ulster), 1,500 of Baillie`s Lowland infantry and a few cannon. If Montrose marched on to Kilcumin (now Fort Augustus), as he intended, he would be placing himself in the centre of a trap. Although urged to withdraw east through Glencoe, Montrose`s only doubt was over which enemy army to attack first. Joined by Duncan Mor Stewart, 8th of Appin, Duncan, 2nd of Ardsheal, Alexander, 4th of Invernahyle, and 200 of their clansmen, Montrose crossed Loch Leven in Stewart boats

Barcaldine Castle

25

and then struck north-east into the Lochaber mountains, for the moment avoiding Inverlochy. The Chiefs of the MacLeans, the Camerons, the MacDonalds of Keppoch, Glengarry and Clanranald, the MacPhersons and the Robertsons were all to rendezvous with him at Kilcumin, bringing vital reinforcements.

The Chiefs duly arrived to find Montrose already at Kilcumin, having heard of Argyll`s landing at Inverlochy. The Chiefs or Clan Tutors had brought nearly as many men as they had promised and Montrose found himself in command of 2,200 picked fighting-men, of whom 1,000 were Ulstermen. Argyll, when his scouts brought him the news, was angry at the royalist re-enforcements, but then pleased that Montrose had walked into the trap. Either Montrose, who had by-passed Inverlochy already, would march north up Loch Ness to besiege Inverness or would cross the Corrieyairack Pass and march against Baillie. In either case, Argyll would follow swiftly and Montrose would be trapped between two Covenanter armies, each larger than his own.

The one outcome that Argyll did not consider was Montrose doubling back and attacking him, which is precisely what Montrose did. The winter had turned severe and there was deep snow. From their start on the early morning of 31 January 1645 till they joined battle at dawn on 2 February, the royalists had no fires, no hot food and little rest. They marched up Glen Tarff, over the high ridge between Tarff andTurrit to Glen Turrit and by Glen Roy to the Spean at Corriechollie, then up the Eoin stream and a tributary and behind Sgurr Finnisgaig to Creag Shail. On that shoulder of Ben Nevis, they could see below them the camp fires of 2,000 hated Campbells. The Lowlanders they scarcely reckoned.

The royalist army camped in the snow and rocks of Craig Shail overnight. As Argyll had anticipated with grim pleasure, they were nearly starving. From Montrose and the Chiefs to the poorest clansmen, all had the same: a small handful of meal mixed with snow or water; but what Argyll did not know was the height of their morale. He himself was in pain from a dislocated shoulder and had gone on board his galley on Loch Linnhe, leaving Duncan Campbell of Auchinbreck in sole command. Argyll thought that the movements on Creag Shail were made by a poor remnant of Montrose`s army, broken by starvation and the intense cold. The intelligent, young Auchinbreck suspected the truth and gave his orders the night before. The 2,000 Campbells were to form his strong centre, supported by his two or three cannon, while the Lowland infantry guarded the wings. Behind them lay Inverlochy castle.

Long before dawn, Montrose placed his Stewarts, MacDonalds, Camerons and others in the centre and divided the Ulstermen between the two wings. While it was still dark, he began his advance. His thirty cavalry, under the Earl of Airlie, followed more cautiously, as a reserve.

Less than half a mile from Auchinbreck`s front line, they halted to wait a few moments for the first light. Then they advanced again and, at the same moment, they were seen and Montrose ordered his trumpeters to salute the Royal Standard. The Campbells were ready in an instant and had begun to charge the royalist centre, but the Stewarts, Camerons and

MacDonalds had the greater impetus and the greater ferocity. Despite being outnumbered, they bit deeply into the Campbell regiments.

The Ulstermen, meanwhile, had rushed even faster against the Lowland wings and struck them before they had fully formed. Although they were outnumbered three to two, the Irish MacDonalds swept both wings away in a few moments. With admirable discipline, they made no pursuit, but turned right and left on the heavily engaged Campbells. The thirty horsemen cut through the Covenanter rear and closed retreat to Inverlochy Castle. The Campbells fought bravely and well, but, though virtually equal in numbers to their combined enemies, they were overwhelmed. Stewarts, Camerons, MacDonalds and MacLeans all had their age-long quarrels with the Campbells and were mad with battle spirit, hunger and vengeance. Auchinbreck was dying when he was taken prisoner, a few chieftains and the wounded were spared and a few men escaped to the hills. Argyll did not wait to see the end of the battle; for the second time that winter, he fled in his galley. There were still Campbell regiments in England or in Ulster, but the majority of the fighting men of Clan Campbell lay dead by Loch Linnhe. Clan Campbell, as a fighting entity, never fully recovered.

The Stewarts of Appin and most of the allied Clans were allowed to go home with their booty (Montrose knew that he had no choice), but with their promise to return, immediately after the sowing, for a spring campaign. Not all the Clans were punctilious about this, but the Stewarts of Appin kept their promise and returned to Montrose in April.

On 9 May, Duncan Mor of Appin, with Ardsheal, Invernahyle and a substantial body of the Clan took part in the dramatic victory of Auldearn. It was very nearly a defeat. Sir John Hurry, an ex-Royalist, now fighting for the Covenanters and Baillie`s second-in-command, managed to approach Montrose`s position in the village of Auldearn, guided by a local Finlayson. A mile away, Hurry ordered his infantry to fire off and reload their muskets, which had been affected by a thick mist. He reckoned without the keen ears of Montrose`s Ulster scouts.

Montrose had over 900 Irish, 600 Highland clansmen and, unusually for him, 300 well-mounted Gordon cavalry, brought to him by Lord Gordon, against the orders of his father, the convinced, but jealous royalist, the Marquis of Huntly. John Hurry had at least half as many men again and both his cavalry and infantry were mainly experienced, regular regiments.

Not expecting an attack, but with plans ready in his mind, Montrose had less than twenty minutes to make his dispositions. The Stewarts of Appin and other clansmen were posted on and behind a low hill to the south of Auldearn, with the Royal Standard to give the impression that they formed the main body. The Ulstermen were hidden in the barns and behind the hedges to the western side of the village, facing Hurry`s approach. The Gordon cavalry were concealed behind Deadman`s Hill, to the south-west of the Highland infantry, so that they would outflank Hurry`s attack. The Covenanter infantry marched along the Inverness-Auldearn track, with the cavalry just to the south, on their right.

The Ulstermen had been given strict instructions not to charge until the enemy began to attack the "false centre". Waiting, however, was not Colkitto`s strong point. As soon as the first two Covenant regiments were approaching (one of them was a Campbell regiment), Colkitto led out his men from hiding and attacked prematurely, thus bringing the whole weight of the enemy infantry on the 900 Ulstermen.

Though fighting with the utmost bravery, the latter were driven back to the outskirts of the village, where fences and hedges helped them enough to make at least a temporary stand.

Montrose, with the Stewarts in the centre, saw how his plan was miscarrying, ordered the Highlanders to stand fast for a few moments and then rode swiftly to the hidden Gordons, who could see only the enemy cavalry, though they could hear a fierce struggle.

"Will you let the MacDonalds have all the glory of the day?", shouted Montrose, his face radiant.

The 300 Gordon cavalry cheered and swept at the gallop over and down the hill to attack the Covenanter cavalry on their flank. The Covenanters, taken by surprise and confused by mistaken orders, fought only for a few moments and then turned and fled from half their numbers.

Montrose galloped back to the Standard and led the Stewarts of Appin, Camerons and Glengarry MacDonalds down their ridge in a roaring charge against the exposed right flank of Hurry`s infantry. The Gordons, meanwhile, had pursued the Covenanter cavalry for only a mile or two and then returned to attack the infantry in the rear. The heroic, if disobedient, Ulstermen turned from a desperate defence to a wild offensive. The Covenanter infantry fought well, but, deserted by their cavalry and by their few hundred Highland levies and almost surrounded, they eventually broke. The leading two regiments (one being Campbell of Lawers) were virtually annihilated; the others suffered heavily in their flight; Hurry escaped only by the excellence of his horsemanship. The Stewarts of Appin had taken part in another of Montrose`s great victories against superior numbers.

With surprisingly light losses and confident that the Gordon cavalry, glorying in their success, would bring in the rest of the Gordons, Montrose sent the western clans to their homes for a few weeks, while he marched into Aberdeenshire. The subsequent battle of Alford, though a victory that destroyed Baillie`s army, was truly Pyrric, for Lord Gordon died in a cavalry charge and - apart from personal grief - Montrose could no longer rely on consistent Gordon support. Lord Aboyne, the wild younger brother, who now commanded the Gordon cavalry and infantry, would do what he felt like doing or what his still jealous father, Huntly, ordered.

In accordance with their commitment, the Stewarts rejoined Montrose at the end of July, still under the command of Appin, Ardsheal and Invernahyle. Frightened by the appalling losses of their infantry at Auldearn and Alford, the Covenanter Estates were meeting in Perth. The Scots Commissioners in London and their Presbyterian allies in the

English Parliament were losing ground to the Independents (a loose alliance of independent Sects) both in politics and in the Army, with Cromwell becoming more influential in both. If the Scots Estates withdrew any more men from their own army in England, it would weaken the Presbyterian position still further.

The Covenanters had one regular army left in Scotland. This they reinforced with many hundreds of recruits from Fife, while the ex-royalist Earl of Lanark began raising another large force in Lanarkshire. The Estates persuaded the reluctant Baillie, the only experienced general they had, to continue in command and then, with great stupidity, appointed a "committee of War", led by Argyll "to guide" their general!

The Covenanter army was too strong for Montrose to attack it at Perth, while it was in a good defensive position, but Montrose manoeuvred round it and then tempted it away by marching slowly west through West Perthshire and Stirlingshire.

Now that Montrose was in the Lowlands and apparently marching on Glasgow, the committee of War was determined to cut him off and destroy his army. Cheered by news that Lanark would joint them with a large force, the Committee ordered Baillie to pursue. Montrose, who had every intention of fighting at the right time and place, kept just ahead of the Covenanters. He crossed the Forth by fords above Stirling and found the site he wanted: an almost semi-circular position on the lip of the hills, defended in front by the hedges and fences of Kilsyth. There, on 16 August 1645, Montrose won the last of his great victories.

To attack this position, the Covenanter army would first have to march in column past their enemy`s front and over broken ground. Baillie, supported by Balcarres, the only experienced soldier on the Committee, stated flatly that this would be absurd. The Committee over-ruled him; Montrose, they said, would never leave a good defensive position to attack a much larger army in the open.

Montrose, who had more cavalry than ever before, 300 Gordons and 200 Ogilvies, under the 60 year old Earl of Airlie, had planned to wait until the whole Covenant army was spread out in front of him. Some MacDonalds on his right, however, prematurely but successfully attacked the first infantry regiment following their cavalry, while a troop of Gordons charged too soon to the left of centre. Rather than lose the opportunity, Montrose ordered his whole line to advance. The Stewarts ran to the support of the MacDonalds and Airlie led his men in a superb charge against the much more numerous Covenanter cavalry. The latter, already in disorder from trying to about turn on rough ground, fought only half-heartedly, and then fled, riding through one of their own infantry regiments in the process. The Ulstermen delivered one of their devastating charges against the centre of Baillie`s army, which had only just turned from column to line and the Stewarts and MacDonalds destroyed what was left of the Covenant van.

The poorly trained Fife levies fled without being attacked, but not before Argyll and his fellow-Committee members had ridden in abject flight from the field, not drawing rein till they reached Queensferry.

There they took ship to Berwick and sent Chancellor Loudon to London to beg for the return of a large part of the Scottish army in England. Lanark, when he heard the news from Kilsyth, also fled to England and his newly raised levies disappeared home.

The very last Covenanter army in Scotland had been destroyed and Montrose was master of the country. On 18 August, he entered a Glasgow, whose citizens, changing sides, warmly welcomed him and, by a timely coincidence, received the King`s commission as Lieutenant-Governor of Scotland, just brought by Sir Robert Spottiswoode, Secretary of State. Camping his army on Hamilton`s rich estate at Bothwell (to avoid any danger to Glasgow), Montrose publicly issued writs for a new Parliament, in the name of the King, and then solemnly knighted Alistair (Colkitto) MacDonald. Edinburgh, Stirling, Linlithgow and other Lowland towns "componed", that is they surrendered to the King`s Governor and paid him thousands of pounds for his army. Montrose did not forget the Covenanter army in England, but, for the moment, the war in Scotland seemed to be over.

Montrose believed that he could not only hold Scotland, but raise a large enough army to enter the North of England, since the King now had left only a tiny field army and a few dozen towns and castles. He allowed the Western Clans, surfeited with Kilsyth plunder, Hamilton cattle and their share of the "componing" cities and towns, to go to their homes, in accordance with Highland custom. They promised to return if Montrose needed them.

Meanwhile, Montrose received from the entirely sincere Royalist, the Duke of Douglas, news of more than 1,000 recruits and received promises of substantial help from the Earls of Home, Roxburgh and Traquair, totalling another 2,000 men. The first two he believed that he could trust; Traquair, he knew, would join whichever side was clearly winning.

He promised to rendezvous at Kelso and, for this purpose, was sure that he could march with only the Ulstermen and the Gordon and Ogilvie cavalry. Unknown to him, David Leslie, the best of the Covenanter generals, had left the Scottish Commander, Lord Leven, together with 3.000 cavalry (almost all Leven had) and was forced marching north, picking up other Scottish cavalry contingents as they rode. Leven, who was besieging Hereford, felt so weakened that he raised the siege and retreated when King Charles approached, though the latter had only 2,000 horse and no infantry at all.

Just before he left for Kelso, Montrose received two blows, which were to prove fatal. Alistair MacDonald announced that he was going to march most of his Ulstermen to Kintyre and regain it for the MacDonalds. His second-in-command, Magnus O`Cahan, a brilliant young soldier, who had commanded the left wing at Inverlochy and demonstrated skill and courage in every battle, refused to leave Montrose. In the end, Alistair MacDonald took rather more than half his men on his private war with the Campbells in Kintyre and left 600 with Magnus O`Cahan.* The second blow was the desertion of Lord Aboyne and the Gordon cavalry. Aboyne had a quarrel with some of

*The Ulster MacDonalds had several times received reinforcements in small numbers so that, despite their losses, they now had over 1,200 men once again.

30

his allies and he may have had a secret message from his father. On a flimsy pretext, he marched more than half Montrose`s cavalry north to his own country.

All this happened after the Clans had returned home. On 5th September, with only 200 cavalry, mostly Ogilvies with a few Douglases, and 600 Ulstermen, Montrose began his march to Kelso, since he could not break his promise of a rendezvous. The 1,000 men of the Duke of Douglas turned out to be ill-armed peasantry, who would not leave their districts, though Douglas himself, an honourable man, joined Montrose with a handful of horse.

A few hours` march from Kelso, when Montrose had been joined only by Traquair`s son and two or three attendants, he heard the dreadful news that David Leslie had crossed the Border, with 5,000 cavalry and several hundred dragoons, and was riding North-West to cut the royalists off from any retreat North. On top of that came a message that the Earls of Home and Roxburgh, with their great manpower, who were supposed to be patrolling the Border, had both allowed themselves to be taken by "surprise" and were now well-treated prisoners.

Montrose decided to turn aside and then outmarch the Covenanter army to the safety of the hills beyond the Forth. He moved to Selkirk, where he and his 200 cavalry stayed in the town, while the Ulstermen camped below in the Philiphaugh, where the Yarrow and the Ettrick marshes gave some protection to the temporary ramparts. They were probably betrayed to Leslie by Traquair`s son, who deserted late that evening. At any rate, Leslie was well enough informed to by-pass the town and attack the Ulstermen by surprise at dawn.

Alerted, Montrose led his cavalry down to Philiphaugh to find 5,000 Covenant troops surrounding O`Cahan`s men. He would have charged through to die with his infantry, but Douglas and Airlie seized his bridle and dragged him from the field, arguing that his life could still be of inestimable value to the King. They escaped back to the Braes of Atholl. Montrose`s annus mirabilis was over, scarcely more than a year after it had begun. He had won decisively many skirmishes and six pitched battles. The Stewarts of Appin had taken part in the three most skilfully won of these: Inverlochy, Auldearn and Kilsyth.

Knowing the skill and bravery of the Ulstermen and anxious to minimise his losses, General Leslie offered Magnus O`Cahan and the surviving Ulstermen, quarter. On those terms, they surrendered, but the Kirk Ministers with the army forced Leslie to renege.

Over the next few days, the Ulstermen - and their women - were butchered. Only Magnus O`Cahan was kept alive for a ceremonial trial and public execution.

In Argyll, meanwhile, the Stewarts of Appin had no alternative but to stay put when they heard the news. They were fortunate over the Covenanter campaign from the Mull of Kintyre up to Loch Etive, as neither General Leslie nor Argyll himself had time to spare for Appin. The Stewarts might have shared the same fate as the MacDougalls. When Colkitto asked for Argyll royalist allies, Iain MacDougall of

MacDougall, a young boy fervently royalist, gave him 200 men, whom Colkitto then squandered by leaving them to garrison Dunavertie Castle in south Kintyre. When the Covenanter army besieged it, the MacDougalls fought well, but lost their only water supply and were forced to surrender. Again at the instigation of the Ministers, the garrison, although Protestant, was massacred, with the sole exception of one boy, saved by General Turner.

Under the protection of the Covenant army, the Campbells took Gylen Castle and sacked it and then the Covenanters besieged Dunollie Castle. The Stewarts watched the northward march of the powerful army come nearer and nearer. Dunollie, however, held out week after week, and, in the autumn of 1647, both Argyll and Leslie felt obliged to return to Edinburgh for a political crisis that was to lead to the Engagement, constructed by Hamilton to bring together moderate Covenanters and Royalists (but not Montrose!) to try to rescue the King.

The remaining Covenanter forces gave the garrison of Dunollie reasonable terms - which were kept - and abandoned any plans for occupying Appin by force. The Estates sentenced Appin to be ravaged "by fire and sword", but Stewart of Ardvorlich intervened with his friend, General Leslie, and the order was rescinded. Instead, Stewart of Appin and Stewart of Invernahyle were attainted and their estates confiscated until the Restoration in 1660.

During Cromwell`s enforced Protectorate (never accepted by the Camerons), Appin at least escaped a Cromwellian garrison, the nearest being at Dunstaffnage and temporarily at Inverlochy.

Gylen Castle

Dunollie Castle

The Revolution of 1688 succeeded both in England and in Scotland for a variety of reasons, but, above all, because King James VII and II lost his nerve. He had been a brave and greatly professional High Admiral of England during the Dutch Wars, but, in 1688, he would not fight the invading William of Orange, even when the large majority of Army units were still apparently loyal. Despite loyal officers, such as Faversham, Commander of the Guards Brigade, and Graham of Claverhouse (Viscount Dundee), commanding the Scottish cavalry, begging him to advance and fight, James would only retreat and, the more he retreated, the more officers deserted to William. James fled to France in December 1688, when the bulk of his people and of the other ranks of his army still resented a largely Dutch army marching across England.*

In Scotland, the position changed much more slowly, even though most of the tiny standing army had gone to England. Not until 14 March 1689, did a Convention of Estates show a decided Williamite majority and not until 4 April did that Convention state that the King had "invaded the fundamental constitution of his Kingdom .... whereby he hath forefaulted the right to the Crown and the throne is become vacant". This was a significantly different constitutional conclusion from that in England.

Before this declaration, in the absence of members representing much of northern and eastern Scotland, Dundee had left Edinburgh, with troops of one of his cavalry regiments, to raise the Highlands for James

VII and II. The Duke of Gordon held Edinburgh Castle with a small garrison for King James.

William of Orange, now firmly established in England as Co-Sovereign with his wife Mary, James's daughter, sent up to Scotland one of his best generals, Hugh MacKay of Scourie, along with two experienced Scottish Regiments from the Dutch Army and two veteran English Regiments to reinforce the four Lowland regiments raised in March and April, 1689.

After several weeks of rapid movement between the Moray Firth and the Tay, capturing Inverness and Perth and many smaller towns, raising arms, ammunition and money for the cause, Dundee called out the loyal clans on 18 May to meet him in Lochaber. With regret, he had to give up hope of extricating the secretly Jacobite cavalry regiment, Livingstone's, from Dundee. Within a week, Dundee had with him in Lochaber about 4,000 fighting men:, including 1,000 MacDonalds, 900 Camerons, 300 Stewarts of Appin, 300 MacLeans, and MacNeills, MacNaughtons, MacLeods, MacLachlans, Frasers and Lamonts. The only major clans not represented were the Campbells and the Grants and Clan Campbell had still not recovered from the terrible losses of 1644-45 and from Argyll's abortive rising of 1685.

After a month of manoeuvring, Dundee sent home most of the clans, but asked them to stay ready to return at a week's notice. MacKay had retired to Perth for the time being. The Stewarts, with full permission, returned to Appin. Robert Stewart, 9th of Appin, the Chief, was only 16 and had been away at college when the first summons came. He readily agreed to John Stewart, 3rd of Ardsheal, acting as Tutor to the Clan. Ardsheal had already seized Castle Stalker and there was no threat of trouble from the Campbells in the south.

A crisis came when Stewart of Ballechin, Chamberlain of the strategically vital Blair Castle, heard that Lord Murray, the Marquis of Atholl's heir, was about to deliver the castle to General MacKay. Ballechin threw a small garrison into Blair Castle and sent urgently for help from Dundee.

As MacKay's army at Perth was much nearer to Blair, Dundee took the appeal very seriously and sent out an immediate summons to the clans. He started for Atholl with such Camerons, MacDonalds and MacLeans as were with him and ordered the rest to meet him at Blair.

Young Robert Stewart was not going to miss any action. With the agreement of Ardsheal, the boy led the 130 clansmen immediately at hand, straight across northern Rannoch, while Ardsheal raised 200 more and followed two days later. With Robert Stewart was James, 5th of Fasnacloich, and four of his sons.

Macaulay wrote that "the Stewarts of Appin, who, though full of zeal, had not been able to come up in time for the battle, were among the first who arrived after it". Macaulay, however, was mistaken. He had read in a Jacobite's contemporary papers that Ardsheal, as Tutor of the Clan, arrived with nearly 200 clansmen two days after the battle. He assumed that this was the whole Stewart of Appin contribution. Appin, Ballachulish and Fasnacloich correspondence and the evidence to subsequent Court proceedings of witnesses, including the Williamite Lieutenant James Colt, one of Dundee`s prisoners, prove that "the young Chief" brought well over a hundred clansmen to Dundee before the battle. Alexander Stewart of Ballachulish, who was slightly wounded at Killiecrankie, wrote to Invernahyle about the battle two or three weeks later.

The 130 Stewarts of Appin brigaded themselves with their close friends, the Camerons, at Killiecrankie. Lochiel was all the more glad to have them, as his last contingent of Camerons had not yet arrived.

Dundee had reached Blair only just in time. On that evening, 26 July, reliable messengers came in with the news that MacKay, with 4,000 regular troops, including two troops of cavalry, was already in Dunkeld and could be in Killiecrankie the following afternoon. Dundee had only 2,000 men with him, though between 2,000 and 3,000 more clansmen were known to be on the way. The few Lowland officers felt either that the Pass of Killiecrankie should be blocked or that the Jacobite army should withdraw to Drumochter and wait for the reinforcements. The Highland Chiefs, however, were unanimously in favour of fighting, against odds of two to one. This was, in any case, Dundee`s first conviction. He did not wish to stop MacKay`s army in the Pass of Killiecrankie. He wished to allow the Williamite army through the Pass and then to annihilate it. The wise Lochiel, supported by the whole Council of War, begged Dundee not to engage in the fighting himself, but to direct it from above, for Lochiel knew that Dundee was the only man capable of winning back all Scotland for King James. Dundee declined, because this was the first time that he had led a Highland army; after this one day, he promised, he would do what the Council so greatly desired. Fatally, reluctantly, the Council agreed.

The next day, 27 July 1689, Dundee led his small army to the higher ridge of Roinn Rhuari and set them out, in clan regiments, above the path along which the Williamite army would have to march. There were wide gaps between the clans, because Dundee wanted to force MacKay to deploy in a long, thin line for fear of being outflanked, whereas he wanted his small force to charge never less than six deep. The Cameron and Stewart of Appin regiment was a little to the left of Dundee`s centre.

Very cautiously and with Convention Highlanders scouting ahead, MacKay of Scourie marched through the easily defensible Pass and emerged on to the narrow haugh alongside the Garry. Highlanders were seen ahead retiring towards Blair.

First came Lauder`s Fusiliers, a half-regiment, then Balfour`s veteran regiment, then two recently raised regiments, Ramsay`s and Kenmore`s then the new, but very strong, Leven`s (now the K.O.S.B.), then MacKay`s own Dutch-Scots regiment and finally an English veteran regiment, Hasting`s (later the Somerset Light Infantry). The two troops of cavalry, Belhaven`s and Annandale`s, were spread out beside the three regiments in the centre. Behind Hasting`s, the Pass was full of a thousand pack mules, with all the army`s supplies and baggage.

Only when the whole of Hasting`s regiment was out of the Pass and the first pack mules were emerging, did Dundee order his forces to advance over the crest and into sight. By that time, Lauder`s Fusiliers were at the farmtoun of Aldclune and Hasting`s more than a mile behind them. At sight of the Jacobites, MacKay ordered a right turn into line and advanced his men up to the ridge above the Garry and the path. As Dundee had foreseen, the Lowland-Dutch-English army was forced to form up only three deep to meet MacKay`s obsession about being outflanked. (Dundee and MacKay had known each other well, years before, in William of Orange`s Army). MacKay had twice as many men and well over half of them were veteran troops, but he had been trapped into an invidious position. His army was in extended order, facing at right angles to his natural line of retreat. An orderly retreat was, in any case, impossible, since the Pass was choked with baggage animals and the Garry was running fast along the back of their line, two or three hundred yards below their ridge. For all MacKay knew, Dundee also had 4,000 men, so an advance uphill on broken ground was equally impossible. He must wait for Dundee to attack.

Dundee was in no hurry. At the moment, his soldiers had the western sun bright in their eyes. In two hours, the sun would be behind the peak of Schiehallion; meanwhile they were out of musket range and could ignore the two or three very light leather guns in the middle of MacKay`s line.

The Highlanders were increasingly impatient to charge, but remained obedient to orders; the Williamite army, though confident of their fire-power, felt their morale slowly drop.

At nearly 8-0 o`clock on that July evening, Dundee gave the order to charge. The clans, with great gaps between them, rushed down, each against a half or a third of a Williamite regiment. The Camerons, with their Stewart of Appin comrades, charged the right wing of MacKay`s. Halfway down the slope, they were met by a tremendous volley of nearly 4,000 muskets which killed over a tenth of the clansmen. Fifty yards from the enemy, they stopped for an instant, the first two ranks with muskets fired, then threw down their muskets, and all ran on so fast that few of MacKay`s men fired a second time before the Highlanders hit half their line. Most had no time to fit in their plug bayonets. The Camerons and Stewarts killed or swept away half of MacKay`s and then, with good discipline, attacked the other half on their exposed flank and began to roll them up. Half of Balfours', reinforced by the retreating Lauder`s Fusiliers, tried to fight their way to the centre only to find that the survivors of Ramsay`s and Kenmore`s and of the two cavalry troops had fled down to the river. Half of Leven`s were still standing their ground firing indiscriminately into the smoke. MacKay galloped up to them, commended their stand and then rode to his own regiment to find that it had ceased to exist. Hasting`s, on the far right were rather more fortunate. The MacNeils opposite them were the smallest Highland regiment and were to be helped by the MacDonalds and the right half of Hasting`s was protected by a high rocks and a burn. The MacNeils swept away part of Hasting`s, but the MacDonalds accidentally passed behind the remainder and saw the irresistible sight of the baggage train in the Pass. The right-hand half of Hasting`s retired

Schiehallion

in good order to the banks of the Garry and then broke up and tried to ford it when they saw a mass of Camerons, Stewarts and Glengarry Macdonalds coming up at the double, broadswords at the ready. No Lowlander who fought at Killiecrankie ever wanted to see a broadsword charge again.

MacKay had been carried back to the Garry with the surviving part of Leven`s. Once there, it was each man for himself. Of 4,000 Williamite troops, Dundee`s 2,000 had killed 2,000 and captured almost 1.000. The remainder escaped, almost all now unarmed, across the Garry.

If a son of Menzies of Menzies, an ally of MacKay`s, had not guided them to Weem, few would have escaped. Even a week later, in Stirling, MacKay had fewer than one thousand men, many unarmed.

For the cause of the Royal House of Stewart, the magnitude of the victory and the supplies, arms and ammunition on a thousand mules in the Pass, were all in vain. As Dundee turned in his stirrups, in the heart of the battle, to direct his small cavalry troop against those ranks of Leven`s which still stood, a bullet struck through the joint of his breast-plate and mortally wounded him. He lived just long enough to know that his victory was overwhelming. But, as Lochiel had foreseen, no one else had the genius to use the victory that Dundee had provided.

With his habitual blindness in politico-military affairs, King James, now in Ireland, had sent none of the cavalry that Dundee needed, but had sent 500 Irish infantry and a Colonel (now General) Cannon to be Dundee`s second-in-command. The slow and ineffectual Cannon now claimed to be Dundee`s successor as Jacobite Commander. The Highland army had lost over 300 dead out of 2,000 and hundreds more wounded, but, two days later, they were reinforced by over a thousand Camerons, Stewarts of Appin and MacPhersons. By early August, they had 5,000 men, all well-armed from the captured material at Killiecrankie. With 5,000 men, Dundee would have been across the Forth within a fortnight. Not till 21 August did Cannon reach Dunkeld, from which MacKay had marched to Killiecrankie in one day. By that time, it was too late.Lochiel, who had fought the Cromwellians to a standstill in the 1650s, would have been most acceptable as Commander to the vast majority of the Jacobites, but he had felt obliged to accept the King`s inept appointment of an unknown and incompetent Irishman.

Meanwhile, the Convention, appalled at the loss of MacKay`s army, sent their best and strongest Lowland regiment to hold the Tay crossing at Dunkeld. This was the Cameronian Regiment (still called The Cameronians, Scottish Rifles, when abolished by an ungrateful Government in 1965), composed of 1,200 fanatical members of the extreme Cameronian sect from Lanarkshire and North Ayrshire. They were well-armed, highly disciplined and well led by the brilliant young Lt. Col. William Cleland. They occupied the small but ancient town of Dunkeld and its great Cathedral, encouraged the civilians to leave and fortified the whole burgh with barricades, breastworks and loopholed walls.

On 21 August, the 5,000 strong Jacobite army at last marched against Dunkeld, which they could have taken bloodlessly three weeks earlier.

The Stewarts of Appin were on the right flank of the semi-circular attack from the Tay to the west of the Cathedral to the Tay to the east of the great bridge. The 300 Stewarts were commanded by the Tutor, John Stewart of Ardsheal. Robert, the young Chief, Ardsheal`s brother, Alexander, Alexander of Ballachulish and James of Fasnacloich commanded companies. Fasnacloich was accompanied by his four sons, Duncan, Alexander, James and Alan. The Stewarts, Camerons and MacPhersons had the most difficult task of attacking the almost impregnable Cathedral, its tower thronged with Cameronian sharpshooters.

All day long, wave after wave of Highlanders threw themselves against the town, gradually, as the day wore on, capturing house after house, street barricade after barricade. 5,000 against 1,200 sound heavy odds, but, when the 1,200 are defending well-prepared positions and are ready to die to the last man, the odds are not too great. Both sides fought with the utmost courage and both sides had ample arms and ammunition.

Colonel Cleland had ordered that any house that could no longer be held should be set on fire. By late afternoon, the whole town was burning and only the Cathedral and the great mansion of the Marquis of Atholl were still held by the Cameronians.

Four times, small groups of Stewarts, Camerons and MacPhersons had penetrated the less strong areas of the Cathedral walls, but withering musket fire and bayonet charges killed the besiegers. In one of these attacks, Colonel Cleland died; in another, his second-in-command died. The second major was killed in the Atholl mansion and command of the battalion devolved on a captain. Scores of Stewarts were killed, including Ardsheal`s brother Alexander, and scores were wounded, including several of the Fasnacloich family. Inspired by their Colonel`s dying words, the Cameronians fought on with no thought of flight or surrender.

As evening wore on, the Jacobites became aware of a shortage of powder. It transpired that Cannon (who had left the direction of the battle to the Clan Chiefs or Tutors) had not brought down the reserve powder from Ballinluig. Sullenly and reluctantly, the Highlanders drew back from the burning town and left the remnants of the Cameronians still holding the Cathedral and the mansion.

The Jacobite army retired, with its many wounded, to Blair. A few days later the Chiefs decided to disperse for the timebeing, but to sign a Bond committing themselves to raise another army a few weeks later. Each Chief undertook to send at least a specified number of fully armed men. So severe had the casualties been at Dunkeld, following on those of Killiecrankie, that Appin could promise only 100 men with certainty and MacDonald of Glencoe could promise only 50.

Leaderless, the Jacobite campaign drifted northwards. The full tally from the Chiefs of the western clans was never called. Finally, on 1 May 1690, on the Haughs of Cromdale, near Grantown, the 1,800 Highlanders remaining were surprised in a night attack by a Government column from Inverness. About 300 were killed and the remainder dispersed. The war in Scotland was over, but there was an infamous epilogue.

Dunkeld Cathedral

The story of the Massacre of Glencoe cannot be treated here and is well-known anyway. What is much less known is that, at the end of 1691, although the Jacobite chiefs had received permission from King James to take the Oath of Allegiance to William and Mary and all of them, except the late-journeying MacIain of Glencoe, had done so, the original plan of Dalrymple of Stair, to which William had agreed, called for a much wider massacre.

William of Orange signed an order, drafted by Dalrymple, ordering large Government forces to converge on the Stewarts of Appin, the Camerons and the Glencoe MacDonalds, to ravage and destroy them and "not to trouble the Government with prisoners".

An English Privy Councillor, later the Duke of Leeds, heard of the plan and protested so vehemently that William cancelled it. However, on hearing that Glencoe had taken the Oath late (he had waited till the last three days and then gone to Fort William, as it was now called, instead of Inveraray), Dalrymple proposed that this very small clan should be "extirpated", as an example to the others. William read it carefully and signed the warrant.

It was not so much the number of the slain that shocked Scotland, but the fact that, after twelve days of hospitality from the MacDonalds, guests had risen up and slaughtered hosts. 38, including the Chief and his wife, were killed by sword or pistol and somewhere between 40 and 80 died of cold and exposure trying to escape through deep snow.

The number of those murdered would have been higher, if many of Glenlyon`s troops had not been so disgusted when the orders were given the previous evening that they dropped hints in the widely dispersed houses. Two, Ensign Kennedy and Corporal Farquhar, deserve to be remembered for refusing outright to obey the order. They were placed under arrest.

Most of the refugees fled over the mountain passes (women and small children on a bitterly cold 12 February) to the head of Glen Creran and into Appin, where the horrified Stewarts did everything that they could for them. About 150 of this party survived.

Far from frightening the other Clans, the Massacre and the treachery and breach of hospitality involved infuriated even Edinburgh Scots. Dalrymple was forced to resign as Secretary of State for Scotland, but William took no action against him and none against Glenlyon.

In 1695, soon after the detailed Report on Glencoe had been accepted by the Scots Parliament, Robert Stewart of Appin, despite having fought at Killiecrankie and Dunkeld, was made a Commissioner of Supply for the County of Argyll. The authorities now wanted to have the 1689-90 war and its aftermath forgotten, but, as will be seen, the new century was not very old when the Jacobites rose again.

The Stewarts of Appin in 1715
and 1745 and the Road to Derby

CHAPTER 4

Either just before or just after 1700, the name Strathgarry again emerges in Stewart of Appin records. There seems to have been little contact between the (originally Appin) Stewarts of Strathgarry and their kinsmen in Appin. Not since the Stewarts of Atholl and the Stewarts of Appin had joined together in the 16th century to avenge a Strathgarry chieftain killed by MacDonalds had there been well-recorded contacts. Around 1700, however, the original Stewarts of Strathgarry appear to have emigrated to the Netherlands. Duncan Stewart, second son of Donald, 5th of Invernahyle, was Episcopalian Rector of Blair Atholl and he appears to have acquired the lands. Certainly, he passed them on to his son, Alexander Stewart, and he, in turn, to his son, Alexander, 3rd of Strathgarry, who was Church of Scotland Minister of Blair Atholl, 1741 to 1780. The House of Invernahyle always seemed to have adventurous sons, who gained properties outside Appin.

In 1710 or 1711, the historic bond between the Stewarts and Clan MacLaren was again invoked. The MacGregors, who had long been rivals to the MacLarens, had suddenly expelled a MacLaren from his farm in Balquhidder. They were by far the stronger clan by this time (despite being proscribed for a century) and the MacLaren chief notified Appin. Robert Stewart of Appin called up 200 well-armed clansmen and marched swiftly down to Balquhidder, where the broadsword was still more highly regarded than the Law Court. The MacGregors came out in arms, but did not feel that they could take on the Stewarts and MacLarens combined. They withdrew from the MacLaren farm, but put a more graceful face on the matter, saying that they and the Stewarts should fight only for the same King - meaning the exiled Stewart, James VIII.

Before coming to the 1715 Rising, it is interesting to note how mixed the tenant holdings had become on Appin estates. In 1715-16, the 4 merks lands of Shuna had the following tenants:

John ban McIlmichell, John beg McIlmichell, Malcolm Carmichael (both forms of the name being used by neighbours), Donald McColl, Duncan Black, Ewan MacLaren, Hew McColl, Older, and Hew McColl, younger*.

On 1 August 1714, Robert Stewart of Appin was summoned to Edinburgh to give security against being pro-Jacobite. He ignored the summons.

The crisis that had arisen had long been expected. The 1707 Treaty of Union had been acutely unpopular in Scotland, during the debates in 1706 and for several years afterwards. Even after Queen Anne and English and Scottish Ministers had done everything that they could to induce a Union , the final vote, on 16 January 1707, showed a significant minority in The Scots Parliament voting against. The Peers voted 42 to 19 in favour of Union; the country gentry voted 38 to 30 in favour; and

* Inveraray Sheriff Court Records, quoted in the September, 1935 issue of the MacColl Society Journal. The Forfeited Estate Papers of the Stewarts of Appin give an almost identical list of tenants.

the Burgesses voted 30 to 20 in favour. No one doubted that the average Scot was against the Union. The more democratic Convention of Royal Burghs showed that the majority of burgh Burgesses appeared to be against the Union. The Jacobites declared, with some truth, that they alone represented an escape from the Union.

While the national grievance of an unwanted Union was still fresh in the minds of most Scots, the Stewart claimant, James VIII and III, had persuaded the French to send him with an expeditionary force to Scotland in 1708. Storms at sea, plus a loss of nerve on the part of French commanders, rendered the expedition useless, to the great indignation of James. Nevertheless, 1714-15 offered as good a chance as 1708. In the eyes of Scots the Union had actually been broken several times by the English Parliamentary majority. In 1711, the Greenshields case saw the House of Lords reverse a decision of the Court of Session, in what Scots believed to be a breach of Article XIX. In 1712, the Toleration Act, though not unwelcome to moderate Presbyterian Ministers, had a sting in the tail, in the form of an Oath of Allegiance, worded to be offensive to most Scots. In the same year, the Patronage Act was undoubtedly a most flagrant breach of the Treaty of Union.

In 1714, Queen Anne, last sovereign of the principal Stewart line, was dying. Her successor, by Act of Parliament, would be a little known German Prince, the Elector of Hanover, simply because his mother, the Electress Sophia, was a daughter of King Charles I`s sister, Elizabeth of Bohemia. To replace the legitimate Stewart with one of their own family - Queen Mary or Queen Anne - was one thing; to replace him with a German prince who could not even speak English was quite another.

Unfortunately for the Jacobites, political considerations were not so simple. It was not a choice between a German prince and a Stewart prince, but between a German Protestant and a Stewart Catholic. In an epoch when many Protestant Scots were still terrified of the Roman Catholic Church, this mattered greatly, but the effects in 1715 have been exaggerated. The Stewarts of Appin were Episcopalian Protestants, their MacColl, Carmichael and Livingston (MacLeay) adherents were either Episcopalian or Presbyterian.

Their Jacobite neighbours and allies, the Camerons, MacDougalls and MacLeans were either Episcopalian or mixed Episcopalian and Presbyterian. So were the Mackintoshes and other Central Highland clans, such as the Murrays, the Robertsons or the Farquharsons. The Campbells of Breadalbane, who rose for the House of Stewart in 1715, were Presbyterian, as were many of the Lowland Peers and volunteers. Only the MacDonalds and some of the Western Isles clans were partly Catholic. The great majority of soldiers in the 1715 Jacobite army were Protestant.

Why did these clans and, in particular, the Stewarts of Appin rise for a Catholic prince? Partly, it was the "Scotland and No Union" argument, which also carried much sympathy in the Lowlands. Mainly, it was the deep felt loyalty of the Highlander for the legitimate King, the Ard Righ. The Appin Clan, as Stewarts, felt this particularly strongly. There was also among Chiefs such as Appin, the hard felt but rarely defined belief that the Scots, as a nation, had been betrayed by a faction. Even the Treaty of Union, passed, albeit by none too great a majority, in the Scots Parliament was thought illicit. In England, sovereignty rested in the Crown in Parliament, but in Scotland, sovereignty rested - and rests to this day - in the Crown in the Community of the Realm. This was well-known; it had been spelled out clearly in the great Declaration of Arbroath of 1320; yet, neither in the 1688-89 Revolution nor in the 1707 Treaty of Union, had the Community of the Realm consented to the vital developments.

Whatever the causes of the 1715 Rising in Scotland, its failure was certainly due to lack of leadership. The Earl of Mar, who had supported the Union (for which he had been apologising since 1710) and who had been Secretary of State for Scotland on the accession of George I, had been sacked by the latter, on Whig advice, and had then contacted James III and VIII. Without consulting any Highlanders, James gave to Mar a patent as Commander-in-Chief in Scotland. On 27 August 1715, Mar entertained a very large "hunting party" at Braemar. Practically every Highland Chief, including Breadalbane, but not, or course, Argyll, was present, along with Lowland peers, such as Nithsdale, Traquair, Southesk, Carnwath and Linlithgow. They unanimously agreed to rise for James VIII. Robert Stewart of Appin was one of the most enthusiastic.

The Chiefs and peers went home to raise their men. General (later Marshal) Wade estimated the Stewart of Appin total fighting strength as 400, but Robert Stewart led to Perth 250 clansmen.* By the time that he arrived, every city and town north of the Forth was in Jacobite hands. By mid-October, Mar had between 11,000 and 12,000 men. Argyll, who had been appointed Commander-in-Chief in Scotland, had only 4,000 men to defend the crossings of the Forth and to defend Edinburgh. Argyll, however, was an experienced professional soldier, who had served for years under Marlborough. He was a good tactician and something of a strategist. His major-general appointment was well deserved, though the civilian Ministers had given it to him for his not very enthusiastic support of the Union.

Unfortunately for the Jacobites, Mar was no soldier at all. He had no military experience and, although not a physical coward, he suffered from an inability to make up his mind and a tendency to vacillate when he thought that he had decided. Several Clan Chiefs and particularly Robert Stewart of Appin, who had fought in two battles, one directed by the brilliant Dundee, and who had demonstrated his ability to act quickly, would have made infinitely better Commanders than Mar, but their King had appointed Mar and that was that.

The most senior, experienced professional soldier on the Jacobite side in Scotland was Brigadier Macintosh of Borlum, who had captured Inverness before joining Mar in Perth. In the most imaginative action of the war, (probably suggested by Borlum himself), Mar sent Borlum across the Forth, with 2,000 men, from the fishing burghs of Crail and Pittenweem to North Berwick and Aberlady, while another 500 men drew off the Royal Navy warships by a slightly earlier false embarkation from Burntisland. Borlum was to join the Border Jacobites, under

The Western Clans, Camerons, Stewarts and some MacDonalds, made a long detour on their way to Perth in order to beseige Inveraray. They could not take the well-defended burgh or castle and soon moved on. One very young man in the Jacobite force was James Stewart, a natural son of Ardsheal. Decades later, the then Duke of Argyll was to use this fact against James Stewart during the latter`s unjust trial, in Inveraray, for the murder of Glenure in 1752.

41

Viscount Kenmure, and then march north to Glasgow. First, however, he made a dash for Edinburgh in the hope of surprising the Castle. That being impossible, Borlum marched rapidly by Duns to join Kenmure.

The Stewart of Appin Regiment, fortunately for them, had remained with Mar, who had made a feint at Stirling to prevent Argyll from pursuing Borlum and had then, for no very effective reason, marched his army back to Perth. Finally, on 10 November, alarmed at hearing that 6,000 Dutch troops were being sent to Argyll, Mar left Perth with 8,000 men to outflank the Government positions at Stirling by crossing the Forth by fords near Gargunnock. Hearing this, Argyll concentrated his men and left Stirling with 3,500 men, nearly all regulars, to intercept the Jacobite march.

On the morning of 13 November, after a long delay, during which Mar had to be cajoled and bullied into fighting by the Highland chiefs, the two armies came into contact with each other on the gentle slopes of Sheriffmuir. By accident, the right wing of each force heavily outflanked the enemy's left. The Stewarts of Appin, along with the Camerons, Gordons and Keppoch MacDonalds were on Mar's left wing. They charged, failed to break the Hanoverian line, and, as they withdrew to make another charge, were attacked on their exposed flank by half of Argyll's cavalry. They fell back in considerable disorder, but without heavy losses. They reformed several times, but each time they were driven back further.

On Mar's right flank, the Glengarry and Clanranald Macdonalds, the MacLeans, the Campbells of Breadalbane, the MacDougalls and the Earl Marischal's Horse had completely defeated Argyll's left wing and driven it back, with heavy losses, beyond Dunblane. In the words of a letter from the Chief of Clan MacDougall, "five regiments of foot and the Black Horse .... was utterly defate".

The two victorious right wings returned to the centre of the field, but Argyll saw that he had no choice but to retreat. Firstly, his smaller army had suffered greater losses (663 casualties) than the larger Jacobite force. Secondly, his left wing had utterly vanished and did not re-appear, whereas the Stewarts and Camerons of Mar's left wing were already straggling back to the field.

Instead of advancing and attacking the surviving Hanoverians before they could withdraw, Mar sat his horse and dithered. Clanranald had been killed in the right wing's victorious charge, but the other clan chiefs begged Mar to clinch the victory by a charge. He refused and allowed Argyll to withdraw his troops in good order. A wounded Highlander was heard to say: "Oh for one hour of Dundee!"

He was right. If Dundee, Montrose or even Prince Charles Edward had commanded that day, the Hanoverian army would have been entirely destroyed and the Jacobites would have crossed the Forth and found Edinburgh undefended.

* Lt. Col. John
Baynes, "The
Jacobite Rising of
1715", Cassell,
1970

Sheriffmuir has usually been called a drawn battle. As Lt. Col. Sir John Baynes has pointed out, it was, in fact, a Jacobite victory which was let slip by Mar's incompetence*. Instead of pressing on to cross the Forth, as originally intended, Mar gave orders to withdraw to Perth. In disgust, many Highlanders went home, though Appin, John, 4th of Ardsheal, Duncan, 7th of Invernahyle and Alexander, 4th of Ballachulish kept their men with the Jacobite army.

On the same day as Sheriffmuir, 13 November, Brigadier Macintosh of Borlum and his Highlanders, who had marched into northern England, after urgent pleas for help from Lancastrian and Cumbrian Jacobites, were forced to surrender. When surrounded at Preston, they had fought bravely all the previous day and were indignant when the English Jacobite leaders decided to surrender. Borlum later escaped from Newgate Prison and became an active Jacobite again.

When it was too late, James VIII and III landed at Peterhead on 22 December. After a short illness and a leisurely journey, he reached Perth, where Mar was still holding the depleted Jacobite army, on 8 January. The Stewart of Appin officers were delighted to kiss his hand and he seemed pleased enough to meet them, but he did not have the personality of his Uncle, Charles II, nor of his son, Prince Charles Edward, 30 years later. His arrival kept the Jacobite army at its 1 January 1716 level, but many Highlanders had gone home since Sheriffmuir and few had rejoined.

On 28 January, Argyll, who had been heavily reinforced and who now had more regular troops than Mar`s total forces, began to advance on Perth. Mar, to whom James still left all military decisions, retreated to Dundee and then to Montrose. The Clans retreated with reluctance; they had always thought that they had won at Sheriffmuir; and they believed that they could still defeat Argyll, given the right time and place. At Montrose, Mar promised the Chiefs that they would make a stand in suitable terrain south of Aberdeen. On 4 February, however, Mar, Huntly and Seaforth boarded a French ship, the "Marie Therese", insisting on James accompanying them.*

The Jacobite army had now reached Aberdeen only to find that their King and their Commander had both vanished. Understandably, more Highlanders left for home. The remainder of the army, including the Stewarts of Appin, evacuated Aberdeen on 7 February and marched via Donside to Badenoch. There the Jacobite force was disbanded. Those who were not known to Government agents were sent home. The Chiefs and many Chieftains, whose arrests had already been ordered, including Stewart of Appin, Cameron of Lochiel and MacDougall of MacDougall, made their way to Bananish, in the Western Isles, where French ships took them into exile.

So ended the 1715 Rising, so much more widely supported than that of 1745 and yet, for all the lives and effort and devotion put into it, so strikingly unsuccessful, because its politician leader did not have the intelligence and courage to make a soldier, like Macintosh of Borlum, its military commander.

The Hanoverian Government in London was restrained and even merciful in 1716. It had survived a rising which could have been infinitely more dangerous. Apart from the Chief``s, no estates in Appin were forfeited. Ardsheal seems to have bluffed his way through. Duncan of

* To be just to James VIII, he was very reluctant to leave, but he was persuaded that it would save unnecessary bloodshed.

Invernahyle, often called 7th of Invernahyle in 1715-16, was not yet chieftain. His elderly father was still alive and stated truthfully that he had not been "out". Fasnacloich may or may not have been at Sheriffmuir (Alexander Stewart, his cousin, certainly was). Alexander, 4th of Ballachulish fought at Sheriffmuir, but seemed to have been overlooked. The authorities were, in fact, only too anxious not to leave too many resentful chieftains, though the Clan Chiefs had to pay the penalty for the Rising.

By 1725, the Government was again alarmed to discover how well-armed the clans still were. An Act of Parliament was passed "for the more effectual disarming of the Highlands in that part of Great Britain called Scotland". The Stewarts, like the other Jacobite clans, were ordered, on 25 September, 1725, to surrender, by 8 October, "all Broadswords, Targets, Poynards, Whingars, Durks, Side Pistols, Guns or any other War-like Weapons". The order was signed by General George Wade, General Officer Commanding in Scotland, who was already busy constructing strategic roads in the Highlands. Numbers of old rusty muskets and swords were handed in; the better weapons went into the thatch of roofs or the floors of barns.

Robert Stewart, 9th of Appin, had his estates confiscated and was forced to remain in exile. His first wife had been a daughter of MacLeod of MacLeod, who had had two daughters, but only one son, who had died as a schoolboy. After her death, Robert Stewart married Anne Campbell of Lochnell, who had one son, Dugald, and six daughters. Robert died in exile in the mid 1730s.

As the Hanoverian Government was being conciliatory at the time, Dugald Stewart, 10th of Appin, had the estates restored to him. Stewart accounts state that "Dugald, 10th of Appin, to whom the estate was restored, was a boy of tender years when Prince Charles unfurled the Royal Standard in 1745". Whether this was a mistake or a "cover up" for the fact that the Chief would not rise with the Clan in 1745, it is difficult to be certain. It is, however, known now that Dugald Stewart of Appin was adult in 1740, let alone 1745, and was married to Mary MacKenzie before 1745.

That this was well-known in Argyll is indicated by the story of Charles Stewart of Ardsheal in "The Dewar Manuscripts".* There is confusion, as for instance, Robert Stewart, 9th of Appin, is said to be still alive, in 1745, though too old to lead the Clan. His only son, Dugald Stewart, was in Edinburgh when Prince Charles Edward landed and positively refused to rise for the Prince. After much argument, the Clan agreed to be led by Charles Stewart of Ardsheal. John Dewar obviously did not realise that Ardsheal would have been Tutor.

* Pages 161-187 " The Dewar Manuscripts", MacLellan, 1964, but collected by John Dewar mainly in the 1850s.

In fact, Ardsheal`s commission as Colonel from James VIII and III was dated 20 May 1739, Robert Stewart having died before then, and Dugald Stewart, 10th of Appin, having received back the estates, was known to be unwilling to rise for the House of Stewart. As Ardsheal was, by hereditary right, Tutor of the Clan when one was needed, this appointment was perfectly regular. The Dewar tale is correct, however, in saying that Appin himself was adult and living in Edinburgh when the Prince landed. His excuse was that the Appin estates had only recently been restored to him by the Hanoverian Government. In fact, they had been restored nearly 10 years earlier.

Charles Stewart, 5th of Ardsheal, was widely known throughout the Highlands as a magnificent swordsman, possibly the best in Scotland. A variety of sources inform us that, in about 1731, while courting Isobel Haldane of Lanrick, he and a cousin passed through Balquhidder on their way home and met Rob Roy MacGregor, who believed himself to be the best swordsman in the country. During an evening`s drinking, Rob Roy insulted Ardsheal and particularly insulted several times Ardsheal`s father for "fleeing" at Sheriffmuir. This was particularly obnoxious, since the Appin Regiment had at least fought at Sheriffmuir, whereas Rob Roy, after promising help to the Jacobites, had kept his 300 men out of the battle altogether. They fought and Ardsheal clearly won, wounding Rob Roy and forcing him to call a halt.

Thanks to Charles, 5th of Ardsheal, the Stewarts of Appin, with their McColl, Carmichael, Livingston, MacInnes, McCombich and Buchanan adherents, were in a greater state of readiness than most clans when news arrived of the landing of Prince Charles Edward. The Prince had raised his standard at Glenfinnan on 19 August 1745 and had been joined by almost 800 Camerons and 400 Keppoch and Clanranald MacDonalds. After two days there, sending out letters and distributing arms, Prince Charles marched, via Kinlochiel and Letterfinlay, to Invergarry, being joined every day by more MacDonalds. On 26 August, at Invergarry, Ardsheal led 260 men of the Stewart of Appin Regiment into the Jacobite camp, together with 120 MacDonalds of Glencoe. Fifty more Stewarts of Appin and some MacDonalds had been left at Corran Ferry to impede the passage of Hanoverian boats up to Fort William. On their way to Invergarry, the Stewarts had received a consignment of 100 muskets and 100 swords (French, not Highland, unfortunately) from the Prince to supplement the arms kept in hiding.

A MacDonald advance guard had meanwhile occupied the top of the Corrieyairack Pass, which Wade had greatly improved with a zigzag road of buttressed traverses. General Cope, who had left Dalwhinnie with his 2,300 men, fully intending to ascend the Corrieyairack himself, heard there that the Prince`s army had already occupied the head of the Pass. Having marched as far as Garva Bridge, he gave orders to turn towards Kingussie and march to Inverness. If there was insufficient shipping there, they would proceed to Aberdeen and take ship for Leith. That he was leaving the Lowlands and Edinburgh open, he was well aware, but he still hoped to bring his army to Edinburgh before the Prince reached the Capital.

On his march south, Prince Charles stopped for five days at Blair Atholl to allow Duke William, Jacobite Duke of Atholl, and the Duke of Perth to call in Jacobite adherents from their wide lands. There or on the road to Perth, the Stewarts of Appin were joined by 60 more men from Appin and by 40 MacLarens, who had marched across from Balquhidder to serve under Ardsheal. This brought the strength of the Stewart of Appin Regiment up to 360 men. The Company Commanders included James, 8th of Fasnacloich, Alexander, brother of Achnacone, Alexander, 8th of Invernahyle, Duncan, uncle of Ardsheal, and Alexander, 4th of Ballachulish. Their sons or brothers were junior officers. Owing to the total loss of the family papers, little more is known about the Stewarts of Achnacone, but at least two of the chieftain`s brothers, Alexander and Duncan, were officers in the regiment and destined to die at Culloden.

On 4 September, Prince Charles entered Perth in triumph and was received with some enthusiasm by the populace. At Perth, the Prince appointed two Lieutenant-Generals: Lord George Murray, brother of Duke William of Atholl, and the Duke of Perth. George Murray, who was 51, had considerable military experience, gained in 1715 and then, in exile, with the Sardinian army. Having been pardoned, he appeared to have settled down to accept the Hanoverian dynasty and, only two weeks earlier, had called on General Cope in Crieff to help with his transport and supplies.

Duke William, however, vouched for the complete sincerity of his reconversion (of which there is not the slightest doubt) and Prince Charles cordially accepted this and warmly welcomed an experienced, professional soldier. The other appointment - the young, civilian Duke of Perth - was less easy to understand. It may well have been "political", in the sense of pleasing the Franco-Irish interests, who preferred Perth as an individual to Murray.

It is necessary to consider briefly Lord George Murray`s appointment, because one of the great tragedies of the Rising was the gradually growing antipathy between Murray and the Prince. Their increasing disagreement was to be the biggest single factor in the military failure of the Forty Five and for the results to the Highlands, including Appin, and to all Scotland.

The Lowland Chevalier de Johnstone, who was aide-de-camp to Lord George Murray, had great admiration for him and believed him to possess military genius. Significantly, however, he added: "He desired always to dictate everything by himself and, knowing none his equal, he did not wish to receive his advice". Yet he was, in effect, second-in-command, not commander-in-chief. His arrogance could be all the more undiplomatic when his Commander was also his Prince and his Regent. There were faults on both sides and those on Prince Charles Edward`s side were greatly accentuated by the Prince`s Secretary, John Murray of Broughton, and by John O`Sullivan, Quartermaster-General, both of whom detested Lord George. A little later, at Carlisle, the Duke of Perth quietly surrendered his Lieutenant-General`s appointment, rather than add to the dissension, but remained a general officer available for any duty. The Clan Chiefs, it should be said, greatly appreciated Lord George Murray`s professional skill and were contemptuous of the Irish Officers who so frequently criticised him.

On 13 September, Prince Charles crossed the Forth at the fords of Frew, well above Stirling, and arrived at Slateford and Gray`s Mill, just outside the capital, on 16 September. Despite the efforts of the newly arrived Brigadier Fowke, nothing would induce the two regiments of Dragoons, Gardiner`s and Hamilton`s, to stand and fight and, without them, the Town Guard and the several hundred Volunteers would not fight either. The Dragoons retreated to Musselburgh; the Volunteers disbanded themselves; and the Town Guard retired to their homes. Lord Provost Stewart (suspected of being a secret Jacobite) and the Bailies, with the approval of the full Council, tried to negotiate a delay, with the knowledge that Cope`s ships were now entering the Firth of Forth. The Prince, not unreasonably, gave them an ultimatum and sent Lochiel, with 1,000 Highlanders to seek a bloodless entry. The Netherbow Port, outside which Lochiel had a strong body, was opened to allow out the second delegation`s coach and, at about 4 0`clock in the morning, in rushed Lochiel`s party, followed by the whole 1,000 men. The capital of Scotland was captured without a shot being fired.

Later that day, 17 September, Prince Charles Edward rode into the Canongate and Holyroodhouse, in great state, surrounded by crowds described as "huge" and "enthusiastically cheering". At the same time, less than 30 miles away, Cope`s troops were disembarking at Dunbar.

Since the Castle was still in Hanoverian hands, held by the Governor, General Preston, with two companies of Lascelles` Regiment and some gunners and veterans, the main Jacobite Army was camped at Duddingston, leaving small garrisons in vital points of the city. There, the 1,200 muskets and ammunition surrendered by Edinburgh were distributed, ensuring that almost all the Prince`s 2,500 men had firearms. They did not wait long. On the morning of 20 September, the Jacobite Army left Duddingston to cross the Esk and to meet Cope`s troops near Tranent.

Finding that the enemy had already crossed the Esk, Cope took up a strong position, just to the East of Preston, facing South-south-east, his front protected by a marsh, which also gave some protection to his left, and his right resting on the high walls of Preston House. George Murray, who had thrown the Camerons and Stewarts forward to seize Birsley Brae, less than a mile to the south of Preston, could see from the summit the strength of Cope`s position. Ker of Graden reconnoitred the edges of the marsh and the broken ground under fire and reported that it would be impossible to cross it without very heavy losses.

The Prince, however, worried that the concentration of his men round Tranent had left the road to Edinburgh open for a night movement by the Hanoverians, ordered O`Sullivan to post the rearguard (who happened by chance to be Athollmen) near enough to the Musselburgh road to be able to prevent movement. Neither of them informed George Murray; who was still with the Camerons and Stewarts. When he returned and found out, he lost his temper completely and was only restrained by Lochiel. This is related simply because it illustrated the difficulty of communication and perhaps of trust that was to bedevil much of the campaign. The Prince may well have been right to take the action, but there was no immediate haste and Murray should have been informed. On the other hand, George Murray should have been able to keep his temper.

At a Council of War, Lord George Murray outlined his plan for a long detour, by a night march to the east, avoiding the whole length of the marsh, and then an attack on the enemy`s left wing over the firm ground from Seton village. This was unanimously approved and preparations ordered. At that point, another awkward situation arose, which, as it had some implications for the field of Culloden, ought to be noticed.

At Perth, warned by some of the Chiefs of the almost superstitious desire of most Highlanders and especially MacDonalds to have the battle place of honour on the right wing, the Prince had sensibly laid down - and required all to accept - that the Clans should draw lots for the allocation of Clan regiments in the front rank. Lochiel had drawn the right flank, with the Stewarts of Appin next to him. The MacDonalds, not withstanding what they had promised at Perth, vehemently advanced their somewhat unhistorical claim "always to have had the right wing since Bannockburn".* Lochiel and Ardsheal, more interested in winning a decisive victory, offered to take the extreme left wing instead and this was gratefully accepted by the Council. The Prince, always cheered by the prospect of action, drank in great friendship with Lord George Murray, before all save the patrols and sentries settled for a good night`s sleep.

As is well known, young Robert Anderson of Whitburgh, who had an intimate knowledge of the area, woke the commanders and offered to lead them by narrow paths, through the marsh, to come out near the enemy`s left flank. From 4.00 am the Highland army in very narrow column followed Robert Anderson; first Clanranald, followed by Glengarry, Keppoch and Glencoe (which would place them on the right); then the Duke of Perth`s men and the MacGregors; then the Stewarts of Appin and finally the Camerons. When this column had debouched and turned to line, the reserves of Athollmen, Menzies and MacLachlans emerged as the second line.

Cope`s men had been alerted by patrols and he had swung round his whole line, so that his left lay towards Cockenzie and his right lay on a ditch edging the marsh. There were 24 companies of infantry from 4 different regiments, two squadrons of cavalry on each wing and two squadrons in reserve. There were several light cannon on the left and six mortars on the right.

The Prince had been very anxious to lead the charge, but had been unanimously persuaded to lead the second line instead. He stayed well in advance of the second line and no more than fifty yards from the cutting edge of the charge. Lord George Murray led the Camerons, Stewarts of Appin and MacGregors and sent them forward the moment the sun rose behind them, leaving the Duke of Perth to follow suit on the right flank. The Stewarts of Appin found themselves charging Guise`s companies and the right hand company of Lascelle`s. Master-Gunner Griffith was first deserted by his few gunners, then by the artillery guard and then by the neighbouring cavalry, as the Cameron regiment, 700 strong, hit the Hanoverian right with enormous impetus. Lees` companies had already begun to retreat when the Camerons were among them, while next to them, the Guise`s and Lascelles` facing the

* As the almost contemporary Barbour made clear, the MacDonalds were in King Robert`s schiltrom, in the centre, at Bannockburn. At Bruce`s great victory of Old Byland, in 1322, the MacDonalds were on the left. At Harlaw (1411) and Inverlochy (1431), the MacDonalds fought against the Scots Crown. At Killiecrankie the question was not raised.

48

Appin Regiment began to disintegrate just as the wave of broadswords struck them.

In vain General Cope and Brigadier Fowke galloped up and down calling for a stand. It was the same story for the whole length of the line. The cavalry fled first, then the infantry. Within 15 minutes of the first shot being fired, the battle was over. Out of about 2,700 Hanoverians, 300 were killed, over 400 wounded and more than 1,500, including 80 officers, surrendered.

Cope`s army had been virtually annihilated. Most of the survivors who escaped were dragoons. With a few of them, Cope rode to Berwick with the dismal news.

The Jacobite losses were only 30 killed and about 70 wounded. The four officers killed included Captain Robert Stewart of the Appin Regiment. Alexander of Invernahyle saved the life of Lt. Col. Allan Whitefoord, who had been fighting bravely against great odds. They became close friends, with far-reaching consequences.

Prince Charles, the Duke of Perth and Lord George Murray all ordered the men to spare lives as much as possible and sent to Musselburgh and Edinburgh to find doctors and surgeons for the wounded of both sides. The treatment of the Hanoverian wounded and prisoners contrasted deeply with the behaviour of the Government troops after Culloden.

Although the Prince had experienced only one week of active service, at the siege of Gaeta (where he had nearly driven his natural cousin, the Duke of Berwick, to distraction by constantly being in the front trenches), he had, throughout his youth, studied military history and theory and had trained himself for long marches on foot and on horseback. He did appear to have an instinct for the correct strategic decision, which, with hindsight, we now know should have been followed in the earlier stages of the war. On the evening of the battle, he proposed to his Council of War that, with the reinforcements due to arrive in Edinburgh in the next two days bringing their troops to well over 3,000, they should immediately strike south in the wake of Cope and the terrified dragoons and should disperse the Hanoverian force which was known to be assembling at Newcastle. The Council, consisting of all Clan Chiefs or Tutors and all other regimental commanders, were almost unanimous in believing that their numbers were still far too low and that they should wait in Edinburgh until they had a field force of more than 5,000, after the deduction of essential garrisons.

On 22 September, the day following Prestonpans, the Highland army marched triumphantly through Edinburgh to the apparent gratification of the populace. The Prince`s Court was set up at Holyrood and a series of brilliant balls was given. Despite his well-known womanising tendencies in later life, the handsome Prince took polite rather than enthusiastic interest in the innumerable ladies who thronged his Court and spent most of each day with his Council or with his troops at Duddingston. His whole being seemed to be concentrated on how quickly he could gather reinforcements to allow him to march South to engage the Hanoverian troops being hastily brought back from Flanders.

In fact, Prince Charles had five weeks to wait before his Chiefs and senior officers felt that a sufficient force had assembled. It was during this period that Prince Charles appointed his namesake Charles Stewart, cousin of Fasnacloich, to be his Purse Bearer, an officer always close to the Regent, and to be Sheriff of Argyll.

On 17 October, Prince Charles, as Regent, had proclaimed that the Parliamentary Union was dissolved and that the Scots Parliament, which had only been prorogued - which happened to be true - would be reinstated with a forthcoming Election. To those who wanted to remain on the defensive in Scotland, the Prince pointed out that the longer the Hanoverian Government was given, the easier it would be for them to concentrate 30,000 or even 40,000 troops against the Jacobites, instead of the latter destroying the different Hanoverian forces in detail. He had also, of course, pledged to his father a restoration in all three Kingdoms.

By the end of October, reinforcements included 600 Ogilivies, 600 more Athollmen, 900 Gordons and their dependants, 400 Macphersons, 120 MacKinnons and 400 men, under Lord Pitshigo, from Banffshire. Although, in traditional Highland fashion, about a thousand Highlanders had gone home with the loot of Prestonpans, the Prince now had a field army of 5,000 foot and 500 horse. There was also news that regular Scottish and Irish Jacobite units of the French Army were actually on the way to Scotland.

The Chiefs and Lowland Colonels now agreed to march into England, though they did ask for early evidence of English Jacobite support. However, to the Prince's great consternation, they declined to agree to march directly against the elderly and pessimistic Marshal Wade's army at Newcastle, which was already 9,000 strong and would soon have 12,000 men. It was widely known that Wade was lacking in any enthusiasm and in any confidence in his army.

Another victory like Prestonpans, in the vicinity of Newcastle, might well have caused a fall of the Government in London. It would certainly have had an enormous effect on Jacobite morale.

With reluctance, Prince Charles accepted Lord George Murray's plan of advancing through Cumberland into Lancashire, which was thought to be a pro-Jacobite county. On the Prince's own advice, it was agreed to advance on Carlisle in two columns, one direct and the other, via Lauder and Kelso, to give Wade the impression that Newcastle was the target. On 9 November, both columns joined three miles from Carlisle.

The Prince's views on Wade and his army were soon proved correct. On receiving on 1st November, an urgent dispatch for help from Colonel Durand, commanding the 500 militiamen from two counties, who formed Carlisle's garrison, Marshal Wade replied that he could not come immediately because of the state of the roads and lack of supplies. On 15 November, Wade left Newcastle with 9,000 regulars, following an appeal from Ministers, to march the 60 miles to Carlisle. On the same day, after all 500 of the militia, who argued that their annual training was now over, had deserted, Colonel Durand could not prevent the Town Council from surrendering. In the two day siege, Carlisle had cost the Jacobite army one man killed and one wounded. On 17 November, Wade had only reached Hexham on snowladen roads. Hearing there of the surrender of Carlisle, he promptly returned to Newcastle, where at least 1,000 of his men reported sick.

From Carlisle, the Prince wished to march through Lancashire, hoping to pick up recruits in the county, and from there direct to London via Derby. Lord George Murray agreed, but added the strongest wish, virtually a proviso, for some significant English support. As the Prince and Lord George were agreed, the Chiefs acquiesced also. Only in Manchester, did the Jacobite army receive more than a handful of recruits.

There, although several hundred Jacobites took to the streets in welcome, only 300 enlisted in the army. For them, the Manchester Regiment was created.

Marshal Wade was now moving south with a little over 9,000 regular troops, while Sir John Ligonier was mustering an army in Staffordshire from 10,000 regulars sent back from Flanders. Finally, the Government was assembling 8,000 men in London, though half of these were militia. As they advanced to Derby, the mainly Highland army was placing itself in the middle of hostile forces totalling 28,000 men. At this point, Prince Charles had only 5,000 men. Nevertheless, the Highlanders had four great advantages, which they knew as they neared Derby. Firstly, their marching speed was at least double that of the best Hanoverian troops. Secondly, the three Hanoverian armies were currently widely dispersed. Thirdly, some degree of Jacobite sympathies had emerged in London. Fourthly, the French had been galvanised by Prestonpans and the march into England and had concentrated 10,000 troops and many ships at Dunkirk for an invasion of the south coast.

At Macclesfield on the evening of 1 December, Prince Charles learned that the Duke of Cumberland, who had taken command of Ligonier's army, was only 17 miles away at Newcastle-under-Lyme with 10,500 regulars, marching to meet the Jacobites. The Prince summoned a Council of War at which it was agreed to make forced marches to place themselves between Cumberland's army and London. Lord George offered to make a feint south-westwards to lure Cumberland north-west, while the Prince led the remainder of the army to Derby. Murray's feint worked most effectively. Cumberland assumed that the Prince was marching towards Wales and brought his main force north from Stafford to Stone, barring the Jacobite route to Wales. Lord George, having driven back Kingston's Light Horse in confusion, wheeled round and marched swiftly to Derby.

Afterwards, the Prince was to regret that he had not insisted on attacking Cumberland's army while it was strung out over many miles. He had only 5,000 men, but they were well-fed, well-equipped and in the highest spirits. At the time, however, London seemed the priority and there he would have to defeat the weakest of the Hanoverian armies, which contained only 4,000 regulars.

Before noon on 4 December, the Jacobite cavalry advance guard entered Derby, a Whig, pro-Hanoverian city, which nevertheless rang its church bells to show that it was not hostile. The Prince, who had marched on foot 26 miles that day at the head of a great column of clan regiments, arrived late in the afternoon. Billets were found in the town for every single man, even it if meant packing thirty or forty men into some houses. The Highlanders were wildly excited, but very well behaved. They were no more than four days march from London and had passed Cumberland`s army, which would take at least twice as long to reach the capital. In front of them was a "last ditch" force, which was composed half of militia. The morale of the rank and file and of most officers was at its very highest, as we know from their letters written in Derby. All the Stewarts of Appin, with the possible exception of Ardsheal himself, fully shared in the army`s feeling of joyous anticipation. Prince Charles, when he went to bed in Lord Exeter`s house, wondered whether to enter London on foot or on horseback. "England", as Marshal Wade, far off at Doncaster, is alleged to have remarked that day, "is for the first comer".

The Stewarts at Falkirk and the Retreat to the North

CHAPTER 5

On Thursday, 5 December, at seven o'clock in the morning, Lord George Murray informed the Prince that a Council of War must be held immediately, as most of the Chiefs and other Regimental Commanders felt that a withdrawal was now necessary. The Prince, still intent on entering London in four days` time, was as astounded as he was horrified. The Council started at eight o`clock and continued, with one break, all day.

To begin with, the Prince stated, with some heat, that he could not contemplate retreat after they had come successfully so far. "Rather than go back, I would wish to be twenty feet under ground!"* He reminded the Council that they had just had confirmation that the first 800 men of the French Army (the French Royal Scots and Irish regimental piquets`) had already landed in Scotland and that his own brother expected to sail with the main French force of over 10,000 men by 20 December.

Lord George Murray spoke for the Chiefs, including Stewart of Ardsheal, who was a cautious man, when not already on the battlefield. Cumberland, he said, was at Stafford, just as near to London, with 12,000 men (a slight exaggeration; he had had definite information the day before that Cumberland had 10,450); Wade, with 10,000 men was marching south in haste; and the Elector, with 8,000 to 10,000 men was in front of them. Their army, he pointed out, was outnumbered by six to one.

In vain, the Prince replied that their Highland marching rate, to which the Lowlanders were now accustomed, would bring them to the

* Captain John Daniel`s Progress with Prince Charles Edward, contained, in full, in "Origins of the Forty Five", Walter Blaikie (Edinburgh).

Elector`s camp at Finchley four full days before Cumberland could arrive; that the Elector`s 8,000 men were believed to be half militia; and that his own men were confident of sweeping the Finchley army away. As for Wade, he was still thought to be in Yorkshire and he was afraid of fighting, as they had already seen.

To the Prince`s horror, all the Chiefs except one agreed with Lord George. In this book, it would be pleasant to say that the exception was Stewart of Ardsheal, but the one who tended to agree with the Prince was a MacDonald, claimed afterwards to be Lochgarry. During the morning session, the Duke of Atholl and the Duke of Perth said little, but were clearly sympathetic to the Prince`s appeal.

The tragic and ironic fact was that, outside the Council, the vast majority of the junior officers and clansmen were of the same opinion as the Prince. This is clear from cheerful letters written the evening before or that morning. Knowing or thinking that they knew a battle to be imminent, the Highlanders thronged the churches to receive the Sacrament and then happily set about cleaning their muskets and sharpening their broadswords. Even the Whig citizens of Derby bore witness to the high morale of the Prince`s men, Cameron or Stewart, MacDonald or Ogilivie, Macpherson or MacLachlan.* Napoleon's famous aphorism, however, "in War, matters of morale are to matters physical as eight to one", had not yet been added to military science.

We now know that what the Prince half guessed, half hoped was correct. There was a panic in London**, according to witnesses such as Henry Fielding and Horace Walpole; hundreds of Jacobite posters were plastered around the centre of the city; and the Prime Minister had shut himself up and was alleged to be trying to judge whether or not to change sides. Until recently, it had long been the fashion for history books to say that, even if they reached London, a mere 5,000 swordsmen would have been swallowed up in the great city. Now historians tend to notice the contemporary evidence that there were a great many Jacobites in London, willing to support, but not to fight, and that the man-in-the-street would have been likely to side with the winner. † Lord George was an experienced soldier, while the Prince had seen only one week of fighting and had read a great deal of military history. Nevertheless, Charles Edward did have the instinct that a Rising that retreats is usually a failing one. For once, the Chiefs were out of sympathy and out of tune with their clansmen. We can only surmise that if the Prince and his Highlanders had marched on, they could have defeated the force at Finchley and a half-willing London could have capitulated, with Cumberland still three or four days of Anglo-Hanoverian marching away.

The second session of the Council showed that all the Prince`s arguments and pleas had been without real effect. The Dukes of Atholl and Perth and possibly one Chief spoke, albeit without much conviction, for the Prince. All the other Chiefs and colonels, including Lochiel and Ardsheal, the loyalest of the loyal, backed Lord George Murray. A despairing Prince suggested marching to Wales, where information

* "The Highlanders, conceiving of first that they were on the march to attack the army of the Duke of Cumberland, displayed the utmost joy and cheerfulness" .... but when they realised the truth of the retreat, ... "nothing was to be heard throughout the whole army, but expressions of rage and lamentation." Chevalier de Johnston, "Memoirs", Page 55

** Fielding wrote that, when the Jacobites reached Derby"... they struck a terror into it "(London)" scarce to be credied."

† Readers interested in this question are urged to read the late Sir Fitzroy MacLean`s "Bonnie Prince Charlie", Weidenfeld and Nicolson (1988). Particularly when reading Pages 120-130, one should bear in mind that Sir Fitzroy had been an experienced Regular and guerilla soldier.

gained at Preston and Manchester indicated considerable support, but the great majority refused.

They must return towards Scotland and meet the 4.000 Highland recruits and 800 regulars believed to be about to march from Perth. Eventually, the Prince gave in. Except for a few days after Falkirk, he was never the same man again.

That night, the news gradually leaked out, probably through the Irish officers, who had been excluded from the Council, but who had had to be told the outcome. The next morning, the rank and file were almost mutinous when ordered to march north. Lord George let it be known that they were marching to fight Wade, but no one believed this when they moved back towards Lancashire. Rumour had it, correctly, that Wade's army was strung out between Wakefield and Doncaster. It would have been better if they had marched against Wade. The latter had 9,000 effective regulars, but they were moving very slowly and the morale of commander and army alike was low. Another victory, on English soil, would have shaken the Hanoverian government to the core. Lord George and the Chiefs, however, had made up their minds to meet the reinforcements in Scotland before fighting a pitched battle.

The only fighting on the road to Carlisle was at Clifton, south of Penrith, where the rearguard, comprising the Stewarts of Appin, the Glengarry MacDonalds and the MacPhersons, was overtaken by the leading regiments of the 3,000 cavalry* and dragoons, employed by Cumberland as the only troops capable of overtaking the Jacobites. Even cavalry would not have been able to catch up with the Scots, if the Prince had not insisted that the retreat should be measured and as little like a "flight" as possible.

* John Home "History of the Rebellion in the Year 1745" (London), Page 149, stated 4,000, but Cumberland did not have more than 3,000 cavalry, though he may have sent after them 1,000 mounted infantry.

The three regiments, averaging 350 men apiece, had become remarkably cheerful at taking on up to 3,000 cavalry. It was dark, but the occasional moonlight showed the enemy's approach and the Highlanders were partly shielded by hedges and walls.

The MacDonalds were on the right, with a few of Roy Stuart's men, the Stewarts of Appin in the centre and the MacPhersons on the left. Cumberland sent forward a probing force of 500 dismounted dragoons, which approached the MacPhersons. The latter went through the hedge in front of them and charged the dragoons at great speed, while the other two regiments fired on the English rear and on a party of dragoons trying to outflank Cluny's Regiment.

** Account of Captain MacPherson of Strathmashie, contained in "The Lyon in Mourning". Scottish Academic Press (1975), Pages 86-94, Vol. II.

"We were making our way towards the other hedge", wrote Captain MacPherson of Strathmashie afterwards", the advanced parties of the enemy, being dismounted dragoons met us full in the teeth ..... The General, how soon we had given our little fire, ordered us to draw our broadswords, which was readily done, and then indeed we fell to pell-mell with them. But the poor swords suffered much, as there were no less than 14 of them broke on the dragoons' skull caps ..."** However, the MacPhersons took more than 50 swords from dead dragoons, after the dismounted cavalry had fled. The dragoons lost 60 killed. The MacPhersons had only 3 men killed, but another 10 were lost in the darkness or charged too far and were taken prisoner. The Stewarts of Appin did not lose a man.

Clifton was only a skirmish, but it had two important results. Cumberland made no further attempt to overtake the Jacobite army with his 3,000 cavalry and the MacPhersons, Stewarts of Appin and MacDonalds rejoined their comrades in such high spirits that the morale of the whole army was raised.

At Carlisle, Prince Charles left a garrison of 450 men, 200 remaining members of the Manchester Regiment and 250 Scots. The Prince was advised strongly against this, but argued that the Council had agreed to march back to England when the army had been increased to 9,000 men by the reinforcements advancing from Perth and that the possession of Carlisle Castle would then be invaluable.

Further more, Colonel Townley had told him that the Manchester men would prefer to stay. How the Scots were selected or whether or not some volunteered is not known. They were mainly drawn from Roy Stuart's Regiment, with some Ogilivies and MacGregors (two of the MacGregors, one later to be executed and one to be released, composed the beautiful, tragic song, "The Bonnie, Bonnie Banks of LochLomond"). It is certainly true that Colonel Townley advised the Prince to leave his regiment in garrison, but not at all clear whether or not this was the wish of most officers and men.*

Prince Charles was blamed for leaving a garrison in Carlisle, but he had argued that 400 resolute men could hold at least the castle for weeks, since it would take not less than a month to bring heavy siege guns up from the South, and he would be back within a month at the head of 9,000 men. Oddly, perhaps, no one thought of the Royal Navy, not even the Stewart, MacDonald and MacLean chiefs or chieftain - officers who so often travelled by water. The Jacobites left Carlisle on 20 December; Cumberland began his siege on the 21st; six 18- pounder guns arrived, via the Royal Navy and Whitehaven, on the 28th; and, on the third day of heavy bombardment, Colonel Hamilton, against the wishes of Colonel Townley, felt bound to surrender without better terms than "the King's pleasure". Nearly half the rank and file of the Manchester men escaped by hiding or climbing the walls at night. Nine English Officers, five Scottish officers and a dozen men were later executed and many of the remainder transported, but that was after Culloden. There could be no executions while many Hanoverian officers, none harmed, were in Jacobite hands.

On 5 January 1746, only 16 days after leaving Carlisle, Prince Charles was at Bannockburn, at the head of 9,000 men, their morale all the higher for having heard that Lord Lewis Gordon and Gordon of Avochie, advised by the French Major Cuthbert, had inflicted a defeat on the renegade MacLeod of MacLeod and the Whig Clan Companies, at Inverurie, on 23 December , and driven the Hanoverians back to Elgin. Prince Charles could, therefore, have kept his promise of returning to Carlisle, with 9,000 men within a month of leaving the town, but, on 2 January, he had already heard, to his dismay, that Carlisle had been forced to surrender on 30 December.

While the Jacobite army was in Glasgow, Ardsheal sent Invernahyle and Fasnacloich back to Appin to bring in the latest recruits and to

* Captain John Daniel's Progress with Prince Charles, reprinted in Walter Blaikie's "Origins of the Forty-Five", Pages 186-187.

recall to the colours those who had, in Highland fashion, gone home for a while, rather than "deserting". This intervention was so successful that, when the chieftains returned, they brought with them 120 men, bringing the Appin Regiment back to 360 men.

The Jacobites immediate objective was to capture Stirling and its great castle. Lord George doubted that this was worth much trouble and may well have been right, but Ardsheal, Lochiel and the MacDonald Chiefs disliked the idea that the Jacobite army was south of the Forth, but denied the only bridge at Stirling. As the Jacobite artillery left at Carlisle (it could not be brought across the Esk) had been replaced by French guns, brought with Lord John Drummond`s 800 regulars, there was optimism in the camp, but, although the 500 militiamen in Stirling town surrendered on 8 January, the immensely strong castle held out. The French chief engineer, Monsieur Mirabel de Gordon, proved to be completely incompetent, even to the siting of batteries.

Meanwhile, General Henry Hawley had superseded the elderly Marshal Wade and, while Cumberland went south to organise against a new threat of French landings, he marched to Edinburgh. He arrived there on 6 January, with 8,000 regulars, mostly battalions withdrawn from Flanders, and was joined by 1,000 men of the Argyll and Glasgow militias soon afterwards.

By the 17 January, after trouble with his artillery, Hawley was at Falkirk. Lord George Murray suggested that, rather than wait to be attacked at Plean or Bannockburn, the Jacobites should take the offensive and this was enthusiastically agreed by the Prince. Leaving 1,000 men to mask Stirling, Lord George led the first division by fields and tracks towards the ridge of the Hill of Falkirk and Prince Charles followed with the second division. They had 8,000 men, in high spirits, while Hawley had barely more.

The Prince`s cavalry having created a diversion, to the north, which caused the Hanoverians to stand to arms and then relax over their mid day meal (their General was being lavishly entertained by the beautiful and enthusiastically Jacobite Countess of Kilmarnock), the two divisions of the Prince`s army were marching rapidly south-eastwards towards the 400 foot crest of the Hill of Falkirk. It took two urgent messages to persuade Hawley to leave the Countess`s hospitable table, but, when he did arrive, he ordered his troops up the slope.

The Stewarts of Appin were on the left wing, partly behind a gully that ran down to the north, then came the Camerons, Frasers, MacPhersons, MacKintoshes and MacKenzies, while the right wing consisted of the three MacDonalds regiments of Keppoch, Glengarry and Clanranald. These were the Clan regiments in the first division, led to the field by George Murray. The second division, led by the Prince, comprised the Atholl Brigade, the Gordons and the Ogilvies, with seven battalions between them.

The three MacDonald regiments, arriving first, had naturally taken the right wing, protected on their right by marshy ground. Hawley`s three dragoon regiments, leading the Hanoverians, drew up opposite them and repeatedly made feints to persuade the MacDonalds to fire, but Lord George dismounted, walked up and down the ranks and stringently ordered them not to fire until he gave the word. With admirable discipline, the MacDonalds obeyed.

The Hanoverian infantry, as they came level with the cavalry, formed up on the right of the dragoons: the first line comprising Wolfe`s, Cholmondeley`s, Pulteney`s, the Royals, Prince`s and Ligonier`s. Behind them, the second line had Blakeney`s, Munro`s, Fleming`s, Barrel`s and Battereau`s, with Howard`s in reserve. The Stewarts therefore, had Ligonier`s and Battereau`s notionally opposite them, but, in fact, they were far outflanked by them, though protected by the ravine.

General Hawley now ordered his cavalry to charge in earnest. In very good order, the three dragoon regiments charged the three MacDonald regiments, though at that short distance they could not achieve a gallop. The MacDonalds awaited Lord George`s signal and then, at 10 to 15 yards distance, fired in volley. The result was dramatic. About a hundred troopers were killed or severely wounded; Hamilton`s and Cobham`s Dragoons began to pull back; but half of Ligonier`s penetrated deep into the ranks of Clanranald`s, led by Colonel Whitney, who was killed almost immediately. So close knit were the combatants that the horsemen could hardly use their sabres and the MacDonalds, with no room for the broadsword, took to the dirk for troopers and horses alike. Clanranald himself was trapped under a dead horse until rescued. Then the remainder of Ligonier`s fled.

Hamilton`s and some of Ligonier`s, in flight, disordered the Hanoverian left wing infantry and then disordered the Glasgow militia, who had been left at the foot of the hill. Cobham`s withdrew diagonally north-west, were fired on by the Stewarts, Camerons, Frasers and MacPhersons, and then retreated further behind their own army`s right.

It was now pouring with rain and the Stewarts and their fellow-clansmen could not reload, so threw down their muskets and charged with the broadsword. After one volley, Wolfe`s, Cholmondeley`s, Pulteney`s and the Royals turned and fled and all the second line regiments, except Barrel`s followed their example. To attack them, the Stewarts of Appin and the Camerons had come out from behind the ravine and charged at a slant, missing the three remaining regiments in the poor light. The front line Clan regiments had been followed by the Atholl Brigade and Ogilvy`s from the second line.

Meanwhile, the MacDonalds who had displayed such excellent discipline earlier, now found the temptation too great. With all the cavalry and infantry whom they could see in flight, Clanranald`s and Glengarry's disobeyed George Murray`s repeated commands and pursued wildly down the hill, leaving only Keppoch`s standing firm. The Glasgow Militia, already disturbed by the dragoon`s flight, fled as soon as the MacDonalds reached them.

Major General Huske took command of the three right-wing regiments that had not fled, Prince`s, Ligonier`s and Barrel`s marched them round the southern end of the ravine and up the hill, taking the place of the vanished Jacobite left wing, on which they fired from behind and from the flank. The Gordons, who seem to have received the worst of the fire, retired precipitately, as did some of the Frasers. Lord Lewis Gordon and the Master of Lovat withdrew five miles before learning that they had been the victors.

Cobham`s Dragoons re-appeared on the right and rode beyond the three surviving infantry regiments, but, when the Prince summoned up the Irish Piquets, who had been in reserve, they withdrew back to the infantry. Price`s, Ligonier`s and Barrel`s then retired in good order, down the hill, making straight for Falkirk to avoid the chaos at the bottom. The Argyll Militia, who had been left far to the right rear, had disappeared on seeing how the battle was going. When Cobham`s Dragoons had returned to the battlefied, they had probably threatened the Stewarts of Appin on the way, since Lt. Col. Duncan Stewart and John Stewart had evidence, in 1880, that the Appin Stewarts were "one of the few regiments charged by Hawley`s dragoons, whom they decisively repulsed". The Stewarts would have been on the left of the pursuing clan regiments as the dragoons rounded the southern end of the ravine. It is true that it would have been better if the Stewarts and Camerons had tried to prevent the three surviving English regiments from moving north, but either they did not see them in the pouring rain or they assumed that Ogilvy`s two battalions and the Frasers would deal with them.

Lord George Murray had managed to hold on to Keppoch`s and to bring back under his orders his own Atholl Brigade. With these in good order, he marched down the hill at the head of 1,500 men. He was all for occupying Falkirk and the Prince warmly agreed, but it was now dark and no one knew where the Hanoverians were until Lord Kilmarnock came back from scouting through his own policies and reported that the whole Hanoverian army was retreating in complete confusion along the road to Linlithgow and Edinburgh.

Notwithstanding the general confusion and the retreat of two Highland regiments, it was a very complete victory. The enemy was flying eastwards pell-mell; over 500 Hanoverian troops had been killed, including two Colonels and Sir Robert Munro of Foulis, Chief of the Whig Munros, compared with only 50 Jacobite dead; and hundreds of Government prisoners were taken.

Hawley wrote that he had been beaten by "scandalous cowardice" and, on his return to Edinburgh, hanged 31 of Hamilton`s Dragoons and shot 32 infantrymen for cowardice.

The next day showed the scale of the victory, including the fact that the Hanoverians had abandoned Linlithgow as well as Falkirk, but, unfortunately, the Jacobite senior officers quarrelled as much as if they had suffered a defeat. The Master of Lovat and Lord Lewis Gordon had some difficulty in explaining why they had retreated; Lord George Murray was angry that most of the Left and half of the Prince`s second line had broken ranks and joined in the downhill pursuit; he himself was criticised for allowing two out of his three MacDonald regiments to do the same; Lord John Drummond, who had commanded the diversionary moves, was criticised for not coming back quickly enough to command the Left; and everyone agreed that O`Sullivan had first joined the Left and then, in cowardly fashion, had skulked in the rear. The rank and file were happy enough with a palpable victory and the spoils of the field, but the senior officers were in a thoroughly bad temper as the army returned to Bannockburn and Stirling.

The Prince then succumbed to a serious, feverish cold and spent seven days in bed at Bannockburn House, being nursed by Clementina Walkinshaw, who was, much later, to become one of his mistresses. On 27 and 28 January, Prince Charles and Lord George Murray discussed, in great detail, where and when to fight Cumberland, who was known to be on his way to Edinburgh, with two fresh regiments of foot, two regiments of Horse and a train of artillery. Since Hawley had lost at least 1,000 men in dead and prisoners at Falkirk and as Jacobites in Edinburgh reported that Hamilton`s and Ligonier`s Dragoons had been dismissed in ignominy, this meant that Cumberland had no more than 8,500 men (including the half trained Argyll Militia). Most of these men had been soundly beaten at Falkirk. Prince Charles was utterly confident that the victors of Falkirk could defeat the enemy again and hoped to do this in the historic vicinity of Bannockburn.

He was delighted that Lord George Murray appeared to be in full agreement and was looking at potentially suitable sites.

In fact, George Murray had also been talking to Lochiel, Ardsheal and the MacDonald Chiefs. They were greatly worried by the rate of desertion, many Highlanders apparently having returned home with the plunder of the field of Falkirk. Strangely enough, in clan regiments, they had significantly over estimated the rate of desertion. Lord George then called a meeting of all the Clan Chiefs and appears to have advised a retreat to the Highlands, beyond Drumochter. Ardsheal was a "blaze of energy" on the battlefield, but slow and cautious off it. It is not entirely surprising that he supported the call for another retreat, when Lochiel, whom he admired so much, was in favour.

On 29 January, Prince Charles, expecting a final decision on the best location to fight Cumberland, was handed a formal letter from Lord George and the Chiefs "respectfully" demanding a retreat to the North. This, they explained, was due to the fact that "a vast number of the sol-diers of Yv. R.H.`s army are gone home."* They went on to state that, if H.R.H. should risk a battle while Stirling Castle was still in Hanoverian hands, there would be "utter destruction to the few that will remain".* They did not doubt that they could raise "ten thousand effective Highlanders .... in the spring". This missive was signed by George Murray, Lochiel, Ardsheal, Keppoch, Clanranald, Lochgarry, Cluny, Glengyle and the Master of Lovat. It ended with expressions of utter loyalty.

The Prince was as thunderstruck and appalled as he had been at Derby and, all the more so, since he had understood, only a few hours earlier, that Lord George agreed with him over fighting Cumberland between

* John Home "History", Pages 352-353

Falkirk and Stirling. In two different letters that day, the Prince sought to change the minds of George Murray and the Chiefs. His main points may be briefly summarised:

(a) Why should the victors of Falkirk fly from an engagement with those they had conquered?

(b) How much will a long retreat raise the spirits of the enemy and lower those of friends?

(c) What effect will a further retreat have on the French?

(d) What is to happen to the Lowlanders in the army - are they to be abandoned or to retire to the mountains?

He ended the second letter with the words: "..... I take God to witness that it is with the greatest reluctance and that I wash my hands of the fatal consequences which I foresee but cannot help."*

Lord George and the Chiefs were adamant and an orderly retreat was arranged for 1st February, the day on which Cumberland and his 8,500 men reached Falkirk. Unfortunately, most of the Jacobite army failed to rendezvous east of St Ninian`s, as ordered. They simply retired precipitately to the Fords of Frew during the night and early morning. Lord George was furious and blamed O`Sullivan publicly. It is quite likely, however, that O`Sullivan, for once, was innocent. Hearing that they were to retreat again, without knowing why, the Highlanders had simply withdrawn as fast as they could. Nevertheless, they mustered at Crieff on 2 February, in good order. There it was discovered, to the rage of Prince Charles and the surprise of the Chiefs, that the desertions (including those of 1 February) were less than one thousand, since Falkirk, and that the army still had just over 8,000 men. As Prince Charles pointed out to a heated and quarrelsome Council of War at Crieff, those 8,000 men could have defeated an equal sized army, which was substantially the one that they had already defeated at Falkirk only two weeks earlier.

Eventually, it was agreed that the Clan Regiments led by the Prince, should march North, via Blair Atholl and Badenoch, while the Lowland regiments and cavalry should march via Aberdeen and the East Coast. No doubt the Prince and Lord George Murray were relieved to escape from each other (Lord George having offered to command the East Coast column). Prince Charles was still very angry. He felt that he had now been right three times in major decisions and yet been over-ruled by Lord George and the large majority of Chiefs. Firstly, he had wanted to march against Wade in Newcastle on 31 October and it was now known that Wade`s army was then in bad shape, physically and in morale. Secondly, he had been certain that they should advance from Derby to London and London, it had transpired, was full of those sitting on the fence, as well as of genuine Jacobites. Thirdly, he had wanted to fight Cumberland on 2 or 3 February, and it was now clear that he had had enough troops for that purpose. When consideration must be given to Prince Charles`s misplaced over confidence at Culloden, these three factors must be borne in mind.

* John Home, "History", Pages 353-354

The Prince was marching, with the Clan Regiments towards an
Inverness held by Lord Loudon, MacLeod of MacLeod and 2,000 men of
Loudon`s Regiment and of the Whig Clans. While he was staying at
Moy, with "Colonel" Anne Macintosh and a small guard, the Prince was
almost surprised by a sudden and secret march by Loudon and
MacLeod with 1,500 men. A Macintosh boy from Inverness warned the
royal party just in time and MacLeod of MacLeod was "ambushed" by
the Blacksmith of Moy and four men, from whom the 1,500 retreated in
panic and disorder, the only man killed, as he had foreseen, being
Macrimmon, the MacLeod`s hereditary Piper.

Following this debacle, Loudon and MacLeod decided to evacuate
Inverness, by the Kessock Ferry, and only just escaped as the Jacobite
advance guard entered the town. They lost at least 300 deserters that
day, many of whom voluntarily joined the Prince. A strong Jacobite
force of Frasers, MacGregors and MacKenzies (Clan MacKenzie was
split fairly evenly between the Jacobite Earl of Cromartie and the
Hanoverian Lord Fortrose) was sent to pursue Loudon across Easter
Ross and Cromarty. Unfortunately, it had been deemed politic to place
Lord Cromartie in command and he proved a slow and uninspired
general. After a time, the Duke of Perth succeeded Cromartie and, in
the early hours of 19 March, the Jacobites surprised Loudon, MacLeod
and Lord President Forbes at Dornoch. The three principal
Hanoverians escaped and eventually sought refuge at Dunvegan in
Skye, but what was left of their army was dispersed and several
officers, including Colonel Anne`s husband, the Chief of Clan
Macintosh, were captured or surrendered themselves.

Meanwhile, Inverness Castle`s garrison had capitulated after two days
and the castle was largely destroyed. The aim was now to capture and
destroy Fort Augustus and Fort William. Brigadier Stapleton led a force of
Camerons, Keppoch MacDonalds, MacLeans and Scots-French south-west
for this purpose. Fort Augustus, held by three companies of regulars of
Guise`s Regiments, surrendered after ten days. Stapleton`s troops then
marched on Fort William. This, however, was a much tougher proposition.
Not only did the fort outgun the besiegers, with its eight 12 pounders
and twelve 6 pounders, but it had a garrison of 500 men, half of Guise`s
Regiment and half Argyll Militia, and, above all, it was sustained by the
Royal Navy, which ran in supplies, used its guns on Jacobite positions
and raided MacLean and Cameron territory. It will be recalled that all
the Jacobite heavy artillery had had to be destroyed at the beginning
of the retreat from Stirling (including the guns captured at Falkirk)
and only eight light guns had been brought north.

These were reinforced by 4 pounders, 6 pounders, and mortars taken
at Fort Augustus, but the besiegers had nothing to equal the Fort`s 12
pounders in range and weight. Brigadier Stapleton conducted the siege
as competently as possible with his resources and the Camerons,

MacDonalds and MacLeans, who formed most of his force were grimly determined to rid Lochaber of this terrible thorn in the flesh of their clans.

Most of the Stewarts of Appin stayed, under Ardsheal with the Prince in Inverness, but Invernahyle and Young Fasnacloich were given permission to take parties of Stewarts back to Appin, possibly by rotation, while some Stewarts volunteered to join the besiegers of Fort William.

Appin itself was precariously placed. Castle Stalker, impregnable on its island to a force without artillery, was garrisoned by Argyll Militia with a sprinkling of regulars; they were supported by Royal Navy Ships and in constant touch with Fort William. Appin, the Chief, was sitting in his house (when not in Edinburgh), being neutral, and guarded by a few clansmen, who must act as neutrals also. Fifty or so clansmen left to try to protect the lands of the Jacobite chieftains from raids from Castle Stalker would have been totally inadequate if a tacit arrangement had not been reached with Campbell of Airds in the Castle. It was to the Campbell Governor of the Castle that Invernahyle forwarded, on 21 March, the indignant letter from Lochiel and Keppoch of the previous day, complaining bitterly of the burning of Jacobite houses in Ardgour and Lochaber by the Campbell Militia. "We hope to prevail upon his Highness to hang a Campbell for every house that will hereafter be burned by them"*. The Prince, however, refused to allow any of the numerous Campbell prisoners to be hung or punished as a reprisal.

Soon after 26th March, Young Fasnacloich, Invernahyle and the two brothers of Achnacone, who was lying seriously ill, raised every man that they could and marched back to the Prince at Inverness. Brigadier Stapleton gave them the few Stewarts serving with him, as he was already considering raising the siege. His guns simply could not compete with the combined artillery of Fort William and the supporting warships. By 2 April, the Stewart reinforcements had reached Inverness and the Appin Regiment was back at about 320 men, including 39 MacLarens, who had stayed or returned.

Lord George Murray had, in the meantime, visited the Cromarty and Dornoch Firth operations and replaced Lord Cromartie with the Duke of Perth. With the Prince`s consent, he had then marched south with 700 men of the Atholl Brigade, joined forces with Cluny MacPherson and Menzies of Shian, on 15 March, and had planned to capture by surprise, in a night attack, seven of the most important Campbell Militia Posts in Atholl. This was brilliantly done on the night of 16 March, where upon Lord George, with about a thousand men, placed a post on the northern end of the Pass of Killiecrankie and began the siege of Blair Castle. Since the Jacobites had only two, 4 pounder light guns, the castle's capture could be effected only by bluff or starvation and the garrison commander, the foul tempered Sir Andrew Agnew was not likely to give way to bluff. With Cumberland already in Aberdeen, this was no light-hearted excursion in Atholl. 3,000 Hessian infantry, under Cumberland`s brother-in-law, Prince Frederick of Hesse, were known to be approaching Perth. If Blair Castle could be taken, the Jacobites could hold the Pass of Killiecrankie indefinitely. However, before the large

* The full text of the letter and details of its transmission are contained in the "History of the Stewarts of Appin", 1880, Pages 173 - 175.

garrison could be starved out, Lord George received an urgent recall to Inverness, as Cumberland appeared to be ready to leave Aberdeen. On 2 April, the siege was raised and the Jacobites marched north again. Unfortunately, Lord George felt it necessary to leave the MacPhersons to guard the Badenoch passes, but, even if the 400 to 500 MacPhersons had arrived two hours earlier at Culloden, that itself could hardly have saved the battle.

On 8 April, Cumberland left Aberdeen. Including his detached advance guard, he had 9,000 well-armed regulars. He had not wasted the month of March in Aberdeen. His infantry regiments, most of whom had been at Falkirk, were hard trained, especially in how to resist a rapid, Highland charge. One of Cumberland`s officers came up with the suggestion that with veteran troops, trusting each other, a soldier could ignore the enemy immediately to his front and strike with musket and bayonet at the man just to his right front, leaving the first enemy to the soldier on his left. This meant using the bayonet against the side of each Highlander not protected by his target. Cumberland adopted this idea and used it in infantry training.

The first serious natural obstacle was the Spey. Here, the Duke of Perth and Lord John Drummond had 2,500 men. Although there were fords, the river was high and Perth has been criticised for not defending the line of the Spey, at least for a time. However, his orders had been quite specific: to fall back and not to fight a major engagement without most of the remainder of the Prince`s army. Lord George concurred with these orders and regretted that only the Stewarts of Appin, the Atholl Brigade, the Macintoshes and the MacDonalds of Clanranald were immediately available. Urgent messages were being sent out to recall the other Clan Regiments, such as the Frasers, the Camerons, the other MacDonald clans, the MacPhersons and the MacGregors (the Gordon and Ogilvy battalions were among Perth`s troops). As Cumberland`s army marched faster than expected, three Clan regiments did not reach Culloden in time.

The stage was now set for a decisive battle, but one more circumstance must be mentioned. Both the Prince and his Secretary, Murray of Broughton had been ill with fever in March. The Prince recovered in 10 days, but Murray was still very ill. Hitherto, he had secured food and supplies for the army with efficiency, as George Murray, who disliked him, had testified. Now his place was taken by his depute, Hay of Restalrig, who showed slowness and incompetence. For its last two weeks, the Jacobite army was mostly ill-fed.

Culloden and the
Aftermath in Appin

Chapter 6   It is not enough to say that, physically and in morale, the Jacobite Army that fought at Culloden on 16th April was not the army that had beaten Cope at Prestonpans and beaten Hawley at Falkirk. By a terrible irony, it was not even the Jacobite Army of 15th April.

The night attack on the Hanoverian army outside Nairn was a sensible plan, which might well have offset Cumberland`s superiority in numbers, cavalry and artillery. If it had not been feasible, Lord George Murray, supported by Lochiel and Ardsheal, would not have proposed it. It failed for three main reasons and, by failing, made the Jacobites all the more vulnerable the next day. Firstly, owing to the serious illness of Murray of Broughton and the incompetence of his deputy, Hay of Restalrig, most of the men were weak with hunger; although there was a considerable supply of provisions in Inverness, the issue that day had been one biscuit per man. Secondly, a large proportion of the force was tired from recent long marches: from Fochabers, from Atholl, from Fort William, from Dornoch. Thirdly, the well known phenomenon that the rear of a long column has to march faster than the van, if it is to keep up, was made infinitely worse by the fact that the van consisted entirely of fast marching Stewarts, Camerons, Murrays, MacDonalds and Robertsons, while most of the rear were Lowlanders.

By 2 o`clock in the morning, the local Macintosh guides at the point of the first column were still two miles from the enemy camp and the van was supposed half to circumnavigate the camp. Lord George consulted Ardsheal, Lochgarry and Lochiel, all of whom thought that they were already too late. The rear column, whose commanders had repeatedly sent messages asking the van to slow down, were most of them between two and three miles behind, stumbling over the rough ground of the moor, studded with morasses, the Prince urging and cajoling them forward. He himself was apparently inexhaustible, striding up and down the column, but the men were too tired and hungry to respond. Unable to consult the Prince and with the full agreement of Lochiel, Ardsheal and Lochgarry, Lord George gave the order to retire. The Prince was furious, but there was no remedy. The Reveille drums were already beating in the Hanoverian camp.

The army that struggled back to Culloden and threw themselves down for a couple of hours of sleep was now exhausted rather than tired, starving rather than hungry. The Prince, after marching all night,, rode down into Inverness, where Hay of Restalrig seemed to have done nothing, and strenuously tried to organise the movement of the meal supplies to the camp. When he returned and before meeting the Council of War, the Marquis D`Eguilles, the French Ambassador, sought a private audience, fell on his knees to the Prince and begged him not to fight at Culloden, but to withdraw to the hills across the River Nairn. The Prince thanked him, but said that there must be no more retreats.

The same advice came from the Council of War. Lord George, Lochiel, Ardsheal, Keppoch and most of the other Chiefs called for the army to cross the Nairn and, protected by the marshlands from cavalry and artillery, to retire to a position on the edge of the hills. The Prince, supported at first only by the Duke of Perth and the Irish Officers, refused to retreat. He had been right and the Council had been wrong over attacking Wade in Newcastle; English and Welsh Jacobites had said that he had been right and the Council wrong over the retreat from Derby; he had been right and the Council wrong over retreating from Stirling, instead of fighting Cumberland, when the Jacobite army still had 8.000 well-fed, energetic men at Bannockburn. His brave Highlanders, he said, would win again tomorrow. For today, his 6,000 men would have a good rest and a hearty meal, for which provisions were already on the way from Inverness. Cumberland`s army, after yesterday`s celebration of the Duke`s birthday, would not attack them till the next day. To retreat yet again would only dishearten the men and, he pointed out emphatically, a withdrawal across the Nairn would enable Cumberland to occupy Inverness and cut them off from their supplies.

Whether or not the Prince`s arguments would have convinced some of the Chiefs and Colonels is not known. Certainly, the last point about Cumberland seizing their base at Inverness was a valid one. What ensured their reluctant agreement to fight was a sour remark from Brigadier Walter Stapleton, commanding the units from the French Army. "The Scots", he said, "are always good troops till things come to a crisis". Overhearing this, Lochiel, Ardsheal, MacGillivray and the MacDonald Chiefs, lost their tempers, exhausted as they were by days and nights of ceaseless activity, and swore to fight.

The Prince, who had never seen the Highlanders anything but victorious, was full of enthusiasm. He refused to eat some lamb, offered by the Steward of Forbes of Culloden, saying that he would have nothing to eat himself until the army had been fed from the provisions due to arrive from Inverness. He rushed off to tour the camp and encourage the men. On his way out, George Murray begged to be given the right wing for his Atholl Brigade, with the Camerons and Stewarts of Appin next in line. The Prince readily agreed. Then on his rounds of the regiments, he was horrified to discover just how exhausted the men were. It was now too late to change the orders; MacIntosh and Cameron scouts were coming in with news of Cumberland`s approach.

The Prince was reconciled, however, by the fact that reinforcements were at last arriving. A battalion of Frasers, under Charles Fraser of Inverallochie, had arrived and a second, under the Master of Lovat, was due to come in shortly. Some more of Keppoch`s men were reaching Culloden in small groups and it was said that 500 MacPhersons would arrive from Badenoch and 300 Glengyle MacGregors from Dornoch within a couple of hours. Unfortunately, these 800 valuable fighting men, marching as fast as they could, arrived too late.

According to the carefully attempted lists of Patullo, the Jacobite Muster Master, there should now have been 6,000 men (as the Prince had supposed) in the ranks, but only 5,000 or just under could be found.

The remaining thousand were still asleep in bushes or had gone into Inverness or neighbouring hamlets to seek food. In opposition to these 5,000 men, Cumberland had almost 9,000 men, including the now better trained Argyll Militia. The best research seems to show a total Hanoverian strength of 8,820.

On the right of the Prince`s army, a place won for them by George Murray`s pleas, were the so called Atholl Brigade, which had that morning only about 600 men, Murrays, Menzies, Robertsons and Perth`s MacGregors. Next to the extreme right, were the Camerons, about 700 strong, officered by Lochiel`s brothers, nephews and cousins. On their immediate left were the Stewarts of Appin, estimated at 300 strong, including 39 MacLarens (which meant that only between 20 and 40 Stewarts were still asleep or seeking food, a low figure for a Highland regiment). Under Ardsheal, they were in companies commanded by Achnacone`s brother, Fasnacloich the Younger, Invernahyle, Ballachulish the Younger, Ardsheal`s Uncle, Ardsheal`s natural brother James and Captain Donald MacLaren.

On the left of the Appin Regiment were about 300 Frasers under Inverallochie, who formed the first battalion of the Centre, commanded by Lord George Drummond. Next to them was the Macintosh or Clan Chattan regiment, at full strength of over 500 men, being on the edge of their own lands. They were Macintoshes, MacGillivrays and MacBeans, commanded by Alexander MacGillivray of Dunmaglass, on behalf of Colonel Anne, their Hanoverian Chief``s wife. To their left were the Farquharsons and the mixed MacLachlan and MacLean regiment, commanded by Lachlan MacLachlan, with MacLean of Drimnin as Lieutenant Colonel. Then came John Roy Stewart`s small regiment, recruited in Edinburgh and from among prisoners or deserters from the Hanoverian army.

On the left, under the Duke of Perth, were the three MacDonald regiments, standing, right to left, Clanranald, Keppoch, Glengarry. Keppoch`s had been reinforced by the 120 MacDonalds of Glencoe and Glengarry`s (still commanded by Lochgarry) had been joined enthusiastically by over a hundred Grants of Glenmoriston and Glen Urquhart, who had risen against the orders of their Chief. The MacDonald officers had made a last minute appeal to the Prince to form the Right wing, in accordance with the Bannockburn legend, but Prince Charles had simply said that the honour had been promised to Lord George Murray. Lochiel, Ardsheal and Lord George were probably all aware that the claim was imaginary, but, if the MacDonald rank and file believed it, then the effect was the same as if it were historically true. This irritation was, however, far from being a decisive factor in the battle. Glengarry`s and Clanranald`s had been at odds with each other since Angus MacDonald of Glengarry`s accidental death at Stirling, Glengarry`s men still mourning the cheerful young man, and the Clanranalds angry at the execution of the culprit. More important, tired as the new arrivals were, they had to charge 200 to 300 yards further to reach the enemy`s line than the Right Wing had to charge. At the shortest distances estimated, the MacDonald regiments had over 500 yards to cover, while the Camerons, Stewarts and Athollmen had just over 300 yards. This arose because the Jacobites took post first and then the Hanoverians took line at a slight slant. O`Sullivan made no attempt to correct this nor did the MacDonald Chiefs appear to have asked him to adjust the line.

Cumberland had 15 regiments of infantry, 3 regiments of cavalry and the Argyll militia. At first, the infantry deployed into three lines, with 6 regiments in the first line, 5 in the second line and 4 in the third. Cumberland, partly out of respect for the Highland charge, partly, because the Jacobite army, though smaller, slightly outflanked his own, brought Pulteney`s up to the right of the front line and Batterean`s and Howard`s to the right of the second line, leaving only Blakeney`s as a reserve, where the third line had been. He then brought Wolfe`s from the second line and placed it just in advance of Barrel`s on the left of the front rank, at right angles to Barrell`s, so that the regiment, its backs to the stone wall, which extended from Culwhiniac, could enfilade with its volleys, the Highlanders attacking Barrel`s and Munro`s. (See Sketch, Pages 88 and 89) The Hanoverian front line comprised, therefore, Pulteney`s, the Royals, Cholmondeley`s, Price`s, the Fusiliers, Munro`s, Barrels`s and then, at an angle, Wolfe`s. In the narrow gaps between regiments were either two or three guns.

Cumberland split his cavalry between the two flanks, but, on his left, he ordered Kerr`s and half Cobham`s Dragoons to advance into the enclosures and reconnoitre the possibility of attacking the Jacobite flank. Not entirely trusting the Argyll Militia to behave better than at Falkirk, he sent them back to guard the baggage. He may have forgotten or may have tolerated the fact that 140 Campbells of the Militia were scouting the enclosures in advance of the Dragoons.

The battle began with an artillery duel, in which the odds were all in favour of the Hanoverians. It was not that they had so many more guns, but that they were (unlike Prestonpans and Falkirk) expertly manned, by more than 160 professional Officers and men of the Royal Artillery, under Lt. Col. Belford. The Jacobites had only one expert gunner, a mathematician, with amateur gun crews. Within ten minutes, Belford`s guns had knocked out every single Jacobite gun and crew. One Hanoverian battery had been firing all the time not at the Jacobite guns, but at the Prince`s mounted party, on a rise behind the right centre and at the Highland ranks. Now the other batteries began to fire at both the first line and the second line. The Prince, meanwhile, with two men killed near him, had been persuaded to move to his right, but the standard bearer remained where he was.

The Prince has been much blamed for the delay of almost 30 minutes between the first cannon shot and the beginning of the Highland charge. He was hoping against hope - as were George Murray and all the Highland Chiefs - that the Hanoverian army would advance, so that it could be charged while on the move. Cumberland, however, was no Hawley to order a reckless advance and, at the moment, his artillery was doing his own work for him. For ten minutes after the Jacobite artillery had been silenced, the Prince waited for a Hanoverian advance, while the Chiefs kept their suffering men in check. Then, twenty minutes from the opening shot, the Prince sent MacLachlan of MacLachlan Younger galloping down to give the order to charge. Young MacLachlan was killed by a cannon ball on his way to George Murray, but the Prince guessed this only when no move had been made after another five minutes, when he sent O'Sullivan to the right wing. Lord George surrounded by messages from MacGillivray, Ardsheal, Lochiel, Fraser of Inverallochie and others, begging to charge, turned a deaf ear to O'Sullivan, as he later admitted he usually did on the battlefield, and did not even know that he came from the Prince.

Two minutes later, the MacIntoshes would wait no longer and the Clan Chattan Regiment charged. Immediately, at a sign from Lord George, the Stewart, Cameron and Atholl officers gave the order. The Frasers, MacLachlans, MacLeans and Farquharsons followed a moment later. What was surprising, in view of the facts that they had eaten only one biscuit in 36 hours and were exhausted by marching and counter marching, was the speed and ferocity of the charge. Ardsheal, who was, by 1746, often called "lethargic", ran in front of the Appin Regiment, allowing no one to come within five yards of him.

In subsequent generations, many Stewarts of Appin and their allies were to fight for the Crown and to die for the Crown, but, on this day, there passed gloriously, tragically into History the great epic of Appin's faultless loyalty to the dynasty of their kin. For the last time, Clan Stewart of Appin charged for the sake of the Royal House of Stewart. For the last time, after three centuries of alliance, MacLarens of Balquidder ran forward amongst the Appin Regiment. For the last time, the Stewarts of Ardsheal, of Fasnacloich, of Achnacone, of Invernahyle, of Ballachulish led the charge of Stewarts, of McColls and Carmichaels, of MacLeays/Livingstones and McCombichs, of McInnises and McIntyres, of McCormacks, McLarens and others. For the last time, Clan Stewart of Appin charged side by side with Clan Cameron, as they had done for a hundred years, at Inverlochy, at Killiecrankie, at Dunkeld, at Sheriffmuir, at Prestonpans, at Falkirk and now at Culloden.

The MacIntoshes had charged at the 21st, the Royal Scots Fusiliers, but in the sleet blowing in their faces and in the smoke, they unconsciously veered right, converged with the Stewarts and then split up, some moving left and attacking the Fusiliers, others charging Munro's. The Hanoverian gunners had changed from ball to grapeshot and blasted the charging Highlanders. When the running, kilted figures were little more than 30 yards away, the triple lines of infantry began their rolling musketry fire. Contrary to their practice, the Highlanders did not stop to fire their own muskets, but to keep the impetus of the charge, dropped their firearms and closed with broadsword and target as soon as possible.

Miraculously, among the appalling casualties, neither Lord George nor the Colonels of the Stewarts, Camerons, Frasers and MacIntoshes were killed before the Highlanders struck the Hanoverian ranks. Lord George, still mounted, cut his way through the left flank of Barrel's regiment and only managed to control his horse on the edge of Sempill`s. Then, his coat torn to shreds by musket balls and bayonets, his hat and wig knocked off and his sword broken, he saw as he galloped back the critical state of the right wing attack. He rode as fast as possible between Barrel`s and Wolfe`s, past his retreating Atholl men, mown down by Wolfe`s enfilading fire, to try to bring up the Gordons and Ogilvy`s while the Camerons, Stewarts and MacIntoshes were still breaking through the first Hanoverian line.

Both Lochiel`s ankles had been broken by grapeshot. He lay 20 yards from Barrel`s line, propped up on his elbows, sending forward into the fight any Cameron who tried to help him. Alexander MacGillivray of Dunmaglass, leading the Macintoshes, MacGillivrays and MacBeans of Clan Chattan, had cut his way through the Fusiliers, had been wounded, had cut his way through the edge of Bligh`s, had been wounded again and was found dead, his head in a spring behind the Hanoverian lines. Other groups of Clan Chattan, moving left to avoid the Stewart`s line, attacked Cholmondeley`s. Major Gillies MacBean broke right through Cholmondeley`s and, badly wounded though he was , threw himself on the bayonets of Fleming`s. The young Macintosh standard bearer died, the next bearer was killed soon after. The third bearer, seeing that the retreat had begun, tore off the silk and wound it round his body. He and the standard survived and he earned immortality as Donald of the Colours. Eighteen of the twenty one officers leading the charge died in front of or amongst the Hanoverian infantry.

Charles Fraser of Inverallochie took longer to die. His Frasers, aiming originally at the Fusiliers, were squeezed in their charge by the Stewarts and Clan Chattan veering left and right respectively in the smoke and sleet. Some joined Clan Chattan in attacking Price`s, some joined the Stewarts against Munro`s. Inverallochie and a picked group seem to have broken through the right edge of Munro`s, but were all killed or wounded, by the musketry or bayonets of Bligh`s. Inverallochie was still lying there among the piles of Fraser dead, desperately wounded, when General Hawley saw him after the battle. Hawley ordered his ADC, Major Wolfe (of later Quebec fame), to shoot the defiant young Fraser chieftain. Wolfe refused, but a dragoon of Hawley`s shot him dead.

On the left of Clan Chattan, the small combined regiments of MacLachlans and MacLeans had charged towards Price`s, but had been pushed to their left by the swerve of half the Macintoshes. Lachlan MacLachlan, Chief and Colonel, his ADC son already dead, was among the scores shot down before the survivors reached the Hanoverian bayonets. MacLean of Drimnin, the Lieutenant Colonel, one son dead and the other wounded, would not retreat, but died in front of the Royal Scots, after killing at least one soldier. Seventy percent of the MacLachlans and MacLeans are believed to have died at Culloden, the highest proportionate loss among the Jacobites. Some historians have doubted if any Frasers, MacLachlans and MacLeans actually reached the Hanoverian ranks, but John Home, after meticulous research and talking to survivors of both sides, wrote that there was no doubt that some of each of these clans crossed bayonet with broadsword.*

John Home, "History" Page 238

Meanwhile, the Stewarts and Camerons, now partly mixed, had struck Barrel's and the left hand half of Munro's. The battery between the two regiments was captured, the Camerons broke through the centre of Barrel's and the Stewarts broke through Barrel's right wing. Other Stewarts rushed past the captured guns and attacked Sempill's in the second line. Although Highlanders poured through the gaps in Barrel's and most of the regiment had to retreat, they kept their discipline and fell back, platoon by platoon, on the left flank of Sempill's, each of whose three ranks had fired careful volleys at the advancing Camerons and Stewarts. In the carnage in the centre of Barrel's and on its right, the Cameron regimental colour had gone down and was hidden in a pile of dead four or five high. Dugald Stewart, a young kinsman of Ardsheal's, who was the Appin standard bearer, fell dead and another kinsman picked it up, only to be shot dead himself. A McColl seized the colour and carried it forward against Sempill's until he was killed and another McColl seized it from his hand. By then, the fury of the attack had begun to ebb. Stewarts and Camerons fell back from the gap in Barrel's and from the unbroken lines of Sempill's and from the battered left of Munro's. Barrel's, which had stood fast at Falkirk, and Munro's which had fled, both fought well and stubbornly at Culloden, using the bayonet tactics that had been so well taught and drummed in during their weeks at Aberdeen.

As the clansmen fell back, the second McColl bearing the Stewart colour was shot. A MacLeay from Morvern, called Mac-an-t-ledh, tore it from the staff, wrapped it round his waist and saved it from capture. Ardsheal, who had been the first to penetrate the ranks of bayonets and whose superb swordsmanship had killed several infantrymen, cut his way out, his clothing in tatters, but without a significant wound. Another tall and powerful swordsman, Alexander Campbell of Ardslignish*, who had served with the Camerons (they knew this neighbour well as a life long Jacobite), hacked his way out of Barrel's right wing. Four Camerons picked up their wounded chief and hurried back across the moor. As they carried Lochiel past, the 140 Campbells, behind the stone wall fired three volleys at the retreating Camerons and Stewarts and then climbed the wall to attack the Cameron flank. They were so fiercely received, however, that they lost two of their four officers and several men killed or mortally wounded.

At this moment, Lord George Murray came back with Glenbucket's Gordons and Lord Lewis Gordon's regiment, but it was too late. The Stewarts and Camerons, having put everything into their charge, were now in full retreat. The Gordons were too few to go forward on their own. They retreated, in good order, after the clansmen, but, within a few minutes, the surviving officers of the Stewarts and Camerons were placing their own men into more disciplined formation.

Twenty-two Stewart of Appin Officers lay dead on the battlefield, including Ardsheal's uncle and two nephews, Alexander and Duncan, the two brothers of Achnacone, Donald, Invernahyle's nephew, and Ballachulish's son, Alexander. At least eleven more were wounded. It seemed a miracle that Ardsheal, who had charged five yards ahead of

* 4 Campbell Lairds had come out as Jacobites, but three had been taken prisoner at the outset and only Ardslignish reached the Prince's army.

the clan was almost the only officer neither killed nor wounded. The Stewart adherents had fared as badly; 18 McColls, 13 out of 39 MacLarens and 6 Carmichaels had been killed, for example, and 15 McColls, 4 MacLarens and 2 Carmichaels wounded.*

Two factors saved the retreating right wing from even heavier casualties. The first was the devotion of Fitzjames`s and Balmerino`s Horse and the steadiness of Gordon of Avochie`s small battalion. The second was the lack of courage of the Hanoverian cavalry in the Culwhiniac Enclosures. The Campbells had made a breach in the stone wall opposite the Jacobite second line and another breach in the corner of the wall, where it turned south, well behind the second line and opposite the Prince`s position. When the Atholl Brigade survivors, other than some who had joined the Cameron-Stewart attack, came reeling back from the enfilading fire of Wolfe`s regiment, the Hanoverian cavalry, Kerr`s full regiment and half of Cobham`s, at last thought that it was safe to emerge from the Enclosures and charge the disorganised, fleeing Athollmen. On emerging, they found themselves on the edge of a sunken track, a minor, but not formidable obstacle, on the other side of which were the two troops of Fitzjames`s Horse and Balmerino`s which had moved across from the Prince`s hillock to guard the right rear. Just to the left of the Jacobite cavalry was Gordon of Avochie`s understrength battalion. The Hanoverian dragoons had 500 sabres; the two Jacobite troops of Horse together had less than 100; but nevertheless the dragoons did not advance.

The fleeing Athollmen ran past, behind the Jacobite cavalry, and the Stewarts and Camerons, in better order, but still very vulnerable to a flank attack from dragoons, retreated behind Fitzjames`s and Balmerino`s, but still the dragoons stayed on the far side of the sunken track and did no more than fire their pistols. Only when Gordon of Avochie`s, joined by Ogilvy`s, began to withdraw in good order, halting and about facing frequently, did the dragoons cross the sunken track and were promptly charged, with great courage, by one sixth of their number of Jacobite horse. Such odds could not be held and the dragoons soon pursued the infantry. Ogilvy`s and Avochie`s, with great coolness, kept their ranks, halted and gave volley fire, whereupon the dragoons, having tested their mettle several times, rode off to seek easier targets. By this time, the Stewarts and Camerons had been able to form regular columns and were marching off with Pipers playing. Ogilvy`s and Avochie`s regiments followed them, still halting, turning, firing when any dragoons approached.

Meanwhile, on the Jacobite left, the disaster had been even greater. The Duke of Perth ordered the three MacDonald regiments to charge as soon as he saw, through the smoke, the MacIntoshes rush forward. The MacDonald Chiefs and officers repeated the order and the advance began, but it may not have had the speed or verve of the MacIntosh, Stewart or Cameron charges. The principal difficulty for tired and hungry men, however, was that they had 200 to 300 yards extra to cover to reach the ranks of Pulteney`s and the Royals. When the Keppoch MacDonalds slowed down, Keppoch`s example kept them moving, but,

The full list of the Appin Regiment casualties appears at Appendix III page 84

soon afterwards, his brother Donald was killed and then he himself mortally wounded.

The MacDonalds advanced to within 30-40 yards of Pulteney`s and the Royals, suffering terribly from grapeshot from two batteries. Three times the leading Highlanders ran forward within 20 yards, but they never closed. Their three advances and retreats were feints to try to tempt the Hanoverian ranks to break formation and come forward, but they were in vain. The Chevalier de Johnstone, serving with Glengarry`s, saw his friend, MacDonald of Scotus, killed with half his men by his side. Years later, he wrote, "if our right" (i.e. the Stewarts and Camerons) "could only have maintained its ground three minutes longer, the English army, which was very much shaken, would have been still more so by the shock of our left wing ...."* Unfortunately, this was wishful thinking, long after the event. The minority of MacDonalds who had come within 20 yards of the Hanoverian frontline had used their third feint without effect; the majority of MacDonalds were already beginning to retreat when the Camerons and Stewarts pulled back; and the threat of outflanking by Kingston`s and Cobham`s Horse was quite clear. In well ordered ranks, the MacDonalds were not afraid of cavalry, as they had shown brilliantly at Falkirk, but a cavalry charge on the flank of a disordered force, whose advance had failed, was certainly to be feared. The MacDonalds fell back at great speed, taking with them such wounded as they could.

The Irish Picquets and the Franco-Scots Royal opened their ranks for the MacDonalds and then closed them again to deliver volley fire at the approaching cavalry. They were few in numbers, but veteran troops (the Irish Picquets were drawn from the very Irish Regiments that had turned the tide against Cumberland, two years before at Fontenoy). That so many MacDonalds escaped was due to their rear guard action.

The Prince, appalled, saw for the first time, his Highland troops in flight - Right, Centre and Left. He had not the ingrained knowledge of the Highlander to realise that, when defeated, he ran fast to fight another day. Nor did he have the sang-froid of the veteran. For two or three minutes, he seemed to be about to gallop down to join Ogilvy`s or the remnants of the Stewarts and Camerons of the right wing to urge a stand. He may even have thought of following Lord Strathallan`s example and charging to his death. Resisting the urgings of his officers, he sat immobile, tears in his eyes. Finally, O`Sullivan rode up, grabbed the reins and pulled the Prince`s horse away. Later, in his spiteful memoirs, Elcho claimed to have called "Coward" after him, but, a moment later, Elcho himself fled, having tried to take Balmerino with him. Balmerino knew that the Cause of the House of Stewart was lost; he was indifferent as to dying by a bullet or by the headsman`s axe and he turned and rode towards the Hanoverian lines.

John Home, after seeking out all the eye witnesses he could, wrote: "When Charles saw the Highlanders repulsed and flying, which he had never seen before, he advanced, it is said, to go down and rally them. But the earnest entreaties of his tutor, Sir Thomas Sheridan, and others, who assured him that this was impossible, were to leave the field ......

Chevalier de Johnstone "Memoirs", Page 146.

72

their entreaties would have been in vain if General O`Sullivan had not laid hold of the bridle of Charles`s horse and turned him about".* Captain John Daniel, standard bearer, who had just returned, wounded, from Strathallan`s charge, was one of the eye witnesses.

The battle was over; the last serious attempt to restore the House of Stewart was over. The cost to the Jacobites had been appalling, but it would have been much worse, if the Hanoverian cavalry had not been largely kept at bay by cool rear guard work. The dragoons massacred all the single fugitives, wounded and small groups that they could find. When the Hanoverian infantry advanced, they bayoneted any wounded whom they noticed. A few of the wounded were saved that night or the next day, but most died untended or were murdered two days later when two companies of infantry were sent back to the battlefield. The total of Jacobite dead on or near the battlefield is now estimated at between 1,100 and 1,300. This does not, of course, include the hundreds of prisoners, who died of untreated wounds or of sickness and neglect in Government prisons and in rotting prison hulks.

Out of 300 men, the Stewarts of Appin regiment lost 92 dead and 65 wounded (see pages 84 and 85), more than half their total strength in casualties and almost a third in dead. The Camerons lost about 250 in killed, again about a third of their total strength. The MacIntoshes had a slightly higher proportion and the MacLachlan and MacLean regiment, charging a much larger regiment and a battery of guns, are thought to have had two-thirds of their men killed. The other first line regiments had lesser, but still severe losses.

The Stewarts of Appin, most of the Camerons, most of the Gordons and MacIntoshes, the Ogilvy regiment and some MacDonalds marched south to Badenoch, with Lord George Murray. They reached Ruthven in reasonably good order. Most of the MacDonalds, Frasers and Chisholms retreated west down both sides of Loch Ness. The Irish Picquets and the (French) Royal Scots, having defended the fleeing left wing to Inverness, there surrendered formally to Cumberland`s advance guard. As they were an integral part of the French Army, they were the only Jacobite troops to be treated as prisoners-of-war. Their commander, Brigadier Stapleton, died a few days later of wounds received on the only occasion when Kingston`s Horse charged home into their ranks.

There were about 550 prisoners of the Jacobite Army in Inverness the day following the battle, including over 200 in French Service. Few prisoners were taken that day or the next; those found still living, on the moor or nearby, almost all shared the fate of the nineteen badly wounded officers, who had taken shelter in Culloden House, or the twelve wounded Highlanders, who were found in the house of the Lord President`s grieve; all were taken out to nearby walls and shot. Nevertheless, in days and weeks and months to come, the Government managed to acquire a grand total of 3,470 prisoners, most of them soldiers of Prince Charles, but many civilian sympathisers or alleged sympathisers. Their respective fates are mentioned below.

While most of the disciplined survivors of his army were marching to Ruthven, Prince Charles had ridden with a few Irish and Scottish

*John Home
"History",
Pages 239-240.

Officers to Gortuleg and then on to Fort Augustus. The following day he sent an ADC, Andrew Lumisden, to Ruthven with a message for the Chiefs and Colonels there. He expressed the warmest thanks "for their attachment and bravery", but suggested that they now "did the best for their own preservation till there was a more favourable opportunity". Hostile chroniclers later quoted the second part, but omitted the thanks and appreciation. When the Prince`s message arrived, there were rather more than 1,500 Jacobite troops at Ruthven. (The Chevalier de Johnstone, writing years later, thought there were "between four and five thousand", but historians have always found that incredible). The Stewarts of Appin, the Camerons, the Ogilvy regiment and some MacDonalds and MacIntoshes received the message with mixed feelings, but the Chiefs and Lord Ogilvy agreed to disperse the men to their home districts, but to consult again in a few days. The Stewarts, the Camerons and the Clanranald and Glencoe MacDonalds marched, via Invernahavon and Roybridge, to their respective homes.

Two weeks later, the wounded Lochiel, who does not appear to have been at Ruthven, sent out a letter to selected Chiefs calling for an armed rendezvous on 16 May. On 25th May, however, he wrote again to the Chiefs, saying that: "Our assembling was not so general nor hearty as was expected, for clan ranald`s people would not leave their own country and many of Glengarry`s have delivered up their arms; so that but few came with Lochgarry to Invermely".... There was no response from the Master of Lovat and only a few men with Barrisdale, so, "it is now the opinion of Mr Murray, Major Kennedy, Barrisdale and all present that your people should separate and keep themselves as safe as possible, and keep their arms, as we have great expectations of the French doing something for us".

By the time Lochiel`s first, let alone second letter reached Ardsheal, he and Invernahyle were both in hiding and Appin was flooded with 800 Campbell Militia, under Major General Campbell of Mamore.

The war had ended with Culloden, however reluctant some Chiefs were to recognise this. A final comment on the war, may well be drawn from John Home`s History. Home had been an eye witness of Prestonpans and Falkirk, as a Hanoverian volunteer; he had then been a Jacobite prisoner; he was a Whig, but also consciously Scottish; in the years after 1746, he interviewed or corresponded with senior officers on both sides.

"The conclusion of this enterprise was such as most people, both at home and abroad expected, but the progress of the rebels was what nobody expected; for they defeated more than once the King`s troops; they over ran one of the united Kingdoms, and marched so far into the other that the capital trembled at their approach, and, during the tide of fortune, which had its ebbs and flows, there were moments when nothing seemed impossible; and, to say the truth, it was not easy to forecast or imagine anything more unlikely than what had already happened".*

* John Home, "History", Page 2

That is a revealingly frank analysis by a Whig historian, writing in a book dedicated, by Royal consent, to King George II.

The aftermath of the Rising was much less terrible in Appin than in Glen Urquhart, Glenmoriston, Moidart, Morar, Knoidart or most of Lochaber. In all these places and in many others throughout the Central and Western Highlands, civilians, including children, were frequently shot and women raped or murdered. All cattle that could be found were removed and crops deliberately burned. Those Highlanders not shot or hanged could starve to death as far as the Hanoverian Army was concerned. Bligh`s, 20th Foot, under their new Commander, Lord George Sackville, were considered the worst behaved, but Sackville was surpassed for murderous cruelty by two Lowlanders, Captain Carolina Scott of Guises`s and Major Lockhart of Cholmondeley`s. They burned broad swathes through every district they visited, allowed their men to rape and murder as they pleased and shot, with their own hands, neutral Highlanders with Certificates of Immunity.

Although the Stewart of Appin Regiment was one of the two regiments that had done more damage than any other to the Hanoverian Army, little of the atrocious "harrying" took place in Appin. This was mainly because Appin was first occupied by 800 Campbell Militia under the command of John Campbell of Mamore, a man comparatively humane and compassionate. Where his writ ran, atrocities were rarely committed. Only one case of rape was reported in Appin and the girl manged to kill the soldier with a stone, immediately afterwards.

The only two estates confiscated in Appin were Ardsheal and Invernahyle. Although Achnacone`s two brothers had been killed at Culloden, the laird himself, seriously ill, had never left home. James Stewart, younger of Fasnacloich, and his brother John had both been wounded at Culloden, but Fasnacloich himself had not been "out". Ballachulish and his sons had all been "out" and one son had been killed, but Ballachulish somehow convinced the authorities that he had not been in the field. Appin himself was apparently well-known in Argyll for his "neutrality", which was so badly felt by the Clan that they later put it about that he had been a young boy in 1745.

Ardsheal and Invernahyle were too well known and both had to lie in hiding in the hills above their homes. Nevertheless Lady Ardsheal was allowed to go on living for some months in Ardsheal House. Finding that all Ardsheal`s livestock had been removed in the first days of military occupation, Campbell of Mamore returned to Lady Ardsheal her milk cows, 6 wethers, 6 lambs and two bolls of meal, together with a very polite letter, which is still extant. Months later, Captain Carolina Scott arrived with a column of regulars and stole all the livestock, sacked the house and removed all the best timber and stones in his wagon train.

The estate of Invernahyle was mostly saved by the courage of Colonel Whitefoord, whose life Invernahyle had saved at Prestonpans. Hearing, after Culloden, that Invernahyle was listed among those who would never be pardoned, Whitefoord went to the Duke of Cumberland, told him the story of his own rescue and begged for Invernahyle`s life. Cumberland refused. Whitefoord then asked that his estate should be allowed to pass to his wife and son. Cumberland again refused, where-upon Whitefoord laid his commission on the table, as his King could not act with mercy to a beaten foe.

On this occasion, Cumberland was moved to some measure of mercy. He would not have Invernahyle pardoned, but he granted the family's retention of the estate and even gave orders that a guard should be put on Invernahyle House to ensure against looting.

A measure of the comparatively merciful treatment of Appin is the number of Stewart of Appin Regiment prisoners arrested in Appin. Twenty four Stewart of Appin prisoners were taken. Of these, only six were arrested in Appin during the Campbell occupation of May to August 1746 and four of these, all McColls, were probably taken only because two of them had attempted to raid the Campbell camp. The four McColls were all released in 1747; the other two were John McColl, an officer from Portnacroish, who was taken to Carlisle, but appears to have died in prison, and Donald McCormick, who was tried in Carlisle, but acquitted.

Only one soldier of the Appin Regiment was executed. Donald MacDonald of Invernahyle's Company was captured in the Royal Infirmary, Edinburgh, after being wounded at Prestonpans. He was publicly executed at Brampton on 24 October 1746.* Six other Appin prisoners, however, seem to have died of wounds or neglect in prison. Five more, including the Regiment's Quartermaster, were transported. Eleven prisoners were discharged or released under General Pardon in 1747.

One Stewart of Appin Regiment prisoner escaped. He was Captain Donald MacLaren, who was wounded at Culloden, but managed to return to Balquhidder. He was captured in the Braes of Leny, in July 1746, and taken under cavalry escort to Carlisle for trial. In Dumfriesshire, passing the Devil's Beeftub or Anandale's Beefstand, he managed to free himself from the soldier to whom he was tied and threw himself over the precipice, which was shrouded in fog. The soldiers searched, but could not find him. After three days of starving, he began to make his way back to Balquidder, where he lived, disguised as a woman, for two years, until the Act of Indemnity.

The same Act allowed Invernahyle to return home to his unsequestered estate, but, for Ardsheal there was no alternative to exile for life. He had eventually sailed for France in September, 1746. He went into exile at Sens, in Champagne, and was joined by his wife in 1749.

During his many months of hiding around Ardsheal, he had put on a great deal more weight and it may well be that he was suffering from enervating illness. Unlike most Chiefs in exile, he was not able to take a colonelcy in the French Army, but had to remain quietly at Sens. His estate, as noted, had been forfeited to the Crown - the only Appin Stewart estate to be forfeited - and the Crown Factor was Colin Campbell of Glenure, half-brother to Campbell of Barcaldine, who acted for the Barons of Exchequeur. Until May 1752, the Ardsheal tenants paid two different rents, one being a reasonably low rent to the Crown Agent and the other being paid first to Lady Ardsheal and then to Ardsheal in Sens. There was little secrecy about this second rent and Glenure was aware of it and tolerated it. When this illicit rent ceased,

*He was unlucky. Cumberland is believed to have given orders that at least one prisoner from every Jacobite regiment should be publicly executed.

76

with Glenure`s murder in May 1752, followed by the judicial murder of James of the Glen in November 1752, Prince Charles sent 500 livres to Ardsheal and arranged for him to be formally appointed one of the Jacobite Pensioners of King Louis, receiving 3,000 francs a year.

The last and most virulent actions of the Rising`s aftermath in Appin were the murder of Glenure, the trial of James of the Glen in Inveraray and his unjust execution. Many books have been written about Glenure`s murder and about the trial and execution of James of the Glen, natural half brother of Ardsheal. It cannot be dealt with in this short work. Readers interested are recommended to read "The Appin Murder and the Trial of James Stewart", by Lt. Gen. Sir William MacArthur. General MacArthur not only spent a long time in Appin and Lochaber, hearing and sifting opinions and "folk tales", but, far more important, he found a copy of the Precognitions of 120 witnesses or potential witnesses at the trial. To indicate the importance of this, one should note, for instance, that Glenure`s nephew changed his vital evidence as to the clothing of the man he saw on the hillside immediately after the shots, as between his Precognition, shortly after the murder, and his evidence at the trial. The comparison of Precognitions with Trial evidence also discloses the extraordinary and fatal shift in the evidence of John McColl, bowman at Coalisnacoan, and major alterations to the evidence of three McColl relatives, all following months of threats and pressure, while imprisoned at Fort William.

During the months before the confiscation of the estate took effect, James of the Glen had acted as factor for Lady Ardsheal. Glenure, who knew James well, had the good sense to make James his sub factor for the Ardsheal estate. There was "a very good friendship" between James and Glenure and the latter himself described his relations with James as "affectionate". Unfortunately, as was generally the case throughout the British Isles, Glenure, James of the Glen, Allan Breck Stewart and others concerned all drank too much too often and, as with the two Stewarts, uttered meaningless threats during hard-drinking bouts, for which they apologised when sober. Those drunken threats, when witnesses had been forcibly cajoled into quoting them out of context by a ruthless Prosecution, would prove fatal for James.

To Glenure`s misfortune, he had no sub factor like James Stewart in Lochaber, where he was Crown Factor for one of Lochiel`s estates and for Cameron of Callart`s estate. As he was half a Cameron himself, and, through his mother, a cousin of Lochiel, he was the more hated in Lochaber, but also suspected by the Hanoverian authorities of being sympathetic to Jacobites! It was this last suspicion that first caused him to switch James of the Glen from Glen Duror to Aucharn and then caused his decision to evict, with some compensatory arrangements, five tenants from Ardsheal. Even after this plan had been mentioned, James Stewart had still entertained Glenure to a convivial dinner at Aucharn. James of the Glen opposed the eviction by every legal means and might have succeeded. What made the evictions certain was the murder of Glenure.

General MacArthur's book cannot tell us who killed Colin Campbell of Glenure, but it does indicate the innocence of those accused by folktale or popular legend - John, Younger of Ballachulish, James, Younger of Fasnacloich, Donald, nephew of Ballachulish, Red Ewan MacColl and, indeed, Allan Breck Stewart. William MacArthur did not entirely dismiss the possibility (no more than that) of a Cameron or a small group of Camerons having crossed Loch Leven the night before to commit the murder, but, after fighting side by side with the Stewarts of Appin for a hundred years, surely no Cameron in his right mind would commit the murder in Appin, when Glenure had just come over from Lochaber, and then let the Stewarts be blamed. There seems no evidence that a "half witted" Cameron was available to be involved, so the mystery remains. All we know for certain is that James Stewart was innocent, as Lord Cockburn, last century, and Lord Cameron, this century, have so eloquently testified.

Dugald Stewart of Appin's daughter and only child married a wealthy merchant of Leith, but had no children. Appin seems to have spent much of his time in Edinburgh ("gambling" according to the Dewar Manuscripts, but they are totally unreliable). Eventually, having neither heir male in his family nor a grandchild, Dugald Stewart sold the Appin Estate in 1765. Seton of Touch bought the estate in 1769. At least Seton was known to have had Jacobite sympathies. Dugald Stewart of Appin, last of the mainline of his namesake in 1463, died in 1769.

Charles Stewart of Ardsheal, who had been next heir - male, had died in 1757 at Sens. His heir, Alexander, who commanded an East Indiaman made no claim to the title, but, after his death, in 1769, his brother Duncan, 6th of Ardsheal, Collector of Customs for Connecticut, claimed the titles of Ardsheal and Appin in 1771. During the American War of Independence, Duncan of Ardsheal was a loyalist and, in 1781, the estate of Ardsheal was restored to him. There was a delay over the Appin title, but, in 1800, the Lord Lyon King of Arms recognised his son, Charles, 7th of Ardsheal, as "Lorn, Appin and Ardsheal". Today, the present Appin and Ardsheal is descended from Duncan Stewart, son of John, second son of Duncan Stewart, 6th of Ardsheal.

Fasnacloich, Invernahyle, Ballachulish and Ardsheal estates, sooner or later, all had to be sold. Only Achnacone remained in the family which had held it since 1513. Happily, Sir Dugald Stewart of Appin and Ardsheal was able to buy Salachail, in Glen Creran, so their physical link with Appin was restored and preserved.

In 1746, Clan Stewart of Appin ceased to exist as a military and political entity, but the Clan survives, both socially and deep in folk memory, not least among the descendants of the Clan in North America, Australia and New Zealand. Castle Stalker still stands, renovated by a friendly family, and the great beauty of Appin is still there for all to see. Above all, there are still, in Appin, Stewarts and MacColls, Carmichaels and Livingstons, MacInnes and MacCormicks and descendants of all those who fought under the Stewart of Appin banner from Leac-a-dotha and Stalc to Falkirk and Culloden. They and their Kinsmen overseas have a great and noble tradition of which they can be very proud.

❏❏❏

Appendix I — **Descendants of Alan Fitzflaald,** *Ancestor of the Royal Stewarts and of the Stewarts of Appin.*

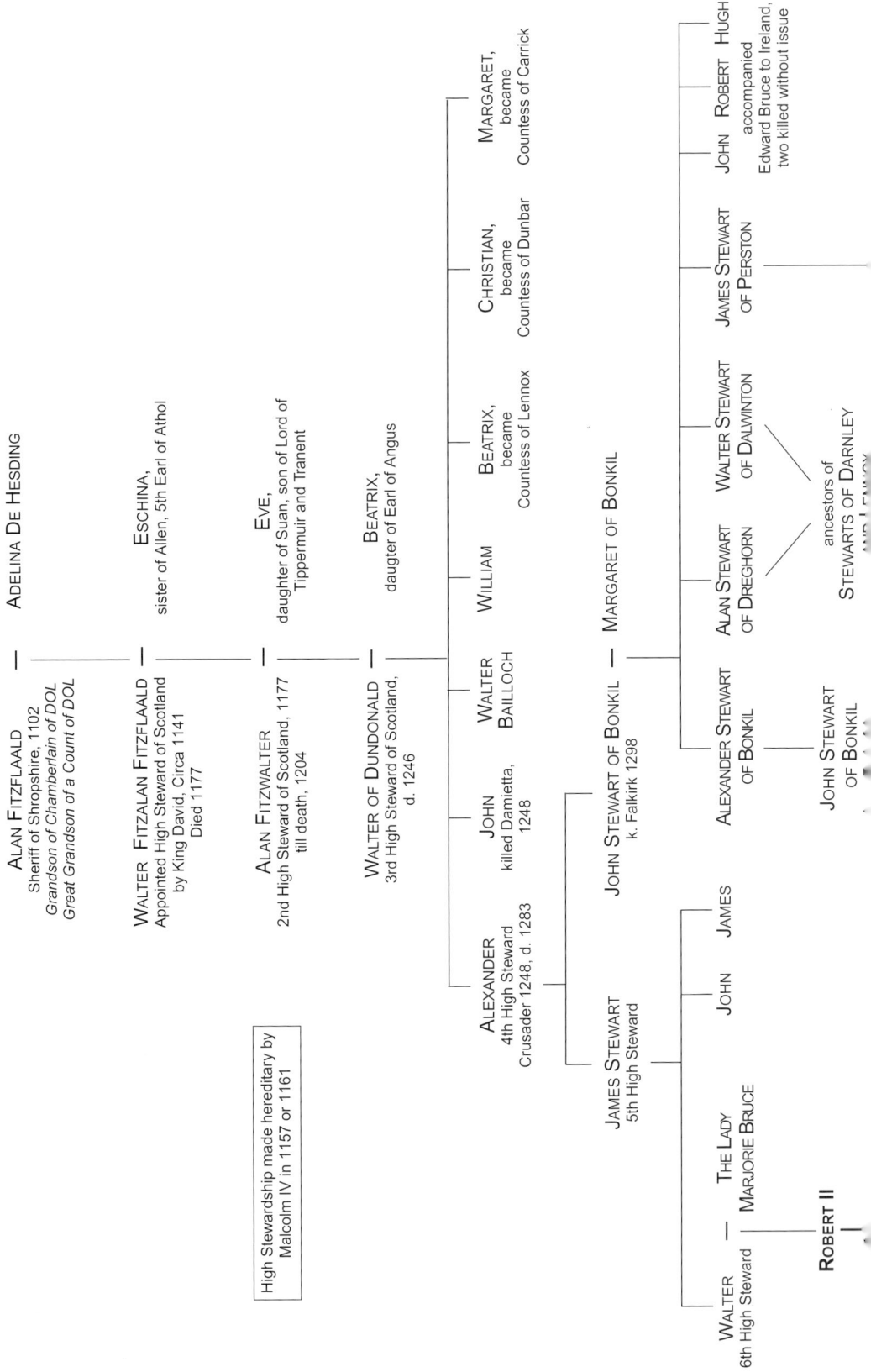

ALAN FITZFLAALD
Sheriff of Shropshire, 1102
Grandson of Chamberlain of DOL
Great Grandson of a Count of DOL
— **ADELINA DE HESDING**

WALTER FITZALAN FITZFLAALD
Appointed High Steward of Scotland
by King David, Circa 1141
Died 1177
— **ESCHINA**,
sister of Allen, 5th Earl of Athol

ALAN FITZWALTER
2nd High Steward of Scotland, 1177
till death, 1204
— **EVE**,
daughter of Suan, son of Lord of
Tippermuir and Tranent

High Stewardship made hereditary by
Malcolm IV in 1157 or 1161

WALTER OF DUNDONALD
3rd High Steward of Scotland,
d. 1246
— **BEATRIX**,
daugter of Earl of Angus

WALTER BAILLOCH | **WILLIAM** | **BEATRIX**, became Countess of Lennox | **CHRISTIAN**, became Countess of Dunbar | **MARGARET**, became Countess of Carrick

ALEXANDER
4th High Steward
Crusader 1248, d. 1283
— **JOHN**
killed Damietta,
1248

JOHN STEWART OF BONKIL
k. Falkirk 1298
— **MARGARET OF BONKIL**

JAMES STEWART
5th High Steward

JOHN | **JAMES**

ALEXANDER STEWART
OF BONKIL
ALAN STEWART
OF DREGHORN
WALTER STEWART
OF DALWINTON
JAMES STEWART
OF PERSTON
JOHN | **ROBERT** | **HUGH**
accompanied
Edward Bruce to Ireland,
two killed without issue

JOHN STEWART
OF BONKIL

ancestors of
STEWARTS OF DARNLEY

WALTER — **THE LADY**
6th High Steward | **MARJORIE BRUCE**

ROBERT II

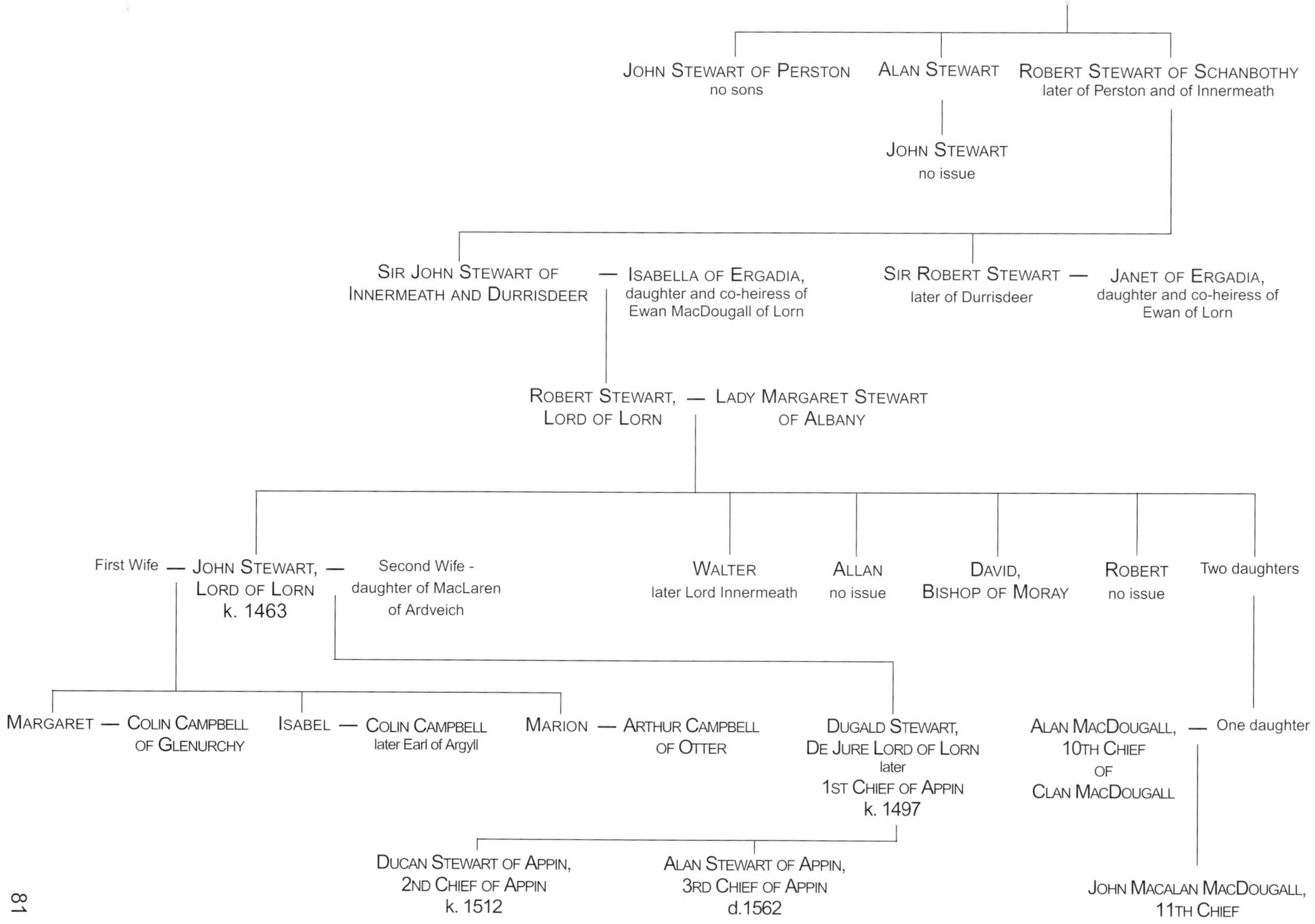

ROBERT STEWART OF SCHANBOTHY
later of Perston and of Innermeath

ALAN STEWART

JOHN STEWART OF PERSTON
no sons

JOHN STEWART
no issue

JANET OF ERGADIA,
daughter and co-heiress of
Ewan of Lorn

SIR ROBERT STEWART,
later of Durrisdeer

ISABELLA OF ERGADIA,
daughter and co-heiress of
Ewan MacDougall of Lorn

SIR JOHN STEWART OF
INNERMEATH AND DURRISDEER

ROBERT STEWART, — LADY MARGARET STEWART
LORD OF LORN   OF ALBANY

Two daughters

ROBERT
no issue

DAVID,
BISHOP OF MORAY

ALLAN
no issue

WALTER
later Lord Innermeath

ALAN MacDOUGALL,
10TH CHIEF
OF
CLAN MacDOUGALL

— One daughter

JOHN MACALAN MacDOUGALL,
11TH CHIEF

DUGALD STEWART,
DE JURE LORD OF LORN
later
1ST CHIEF OF APPIN
k. 1497

MARION — ARTHUR CAMPBELL
OF OTTER

ALAN STEWART OF APPIN,
3RD CHIEF OF APPIN
d.1562

First Wife — JOHN STEWART,
LORD OF LORN
k. 1463

Second Wife -
daughter of MacLaren
of Ardveich

ISABEL — COLIN CAMPBELL
later Earl of Argyll

MARGARET — COLIN CAMPBELL
OF GLENURCHY

DUCAN STEWART OF APPIN,
2ND CHIEF OF APPIN
k. 1512

Appendix II   ## The Stewarts Of Appin - GENEALOGY

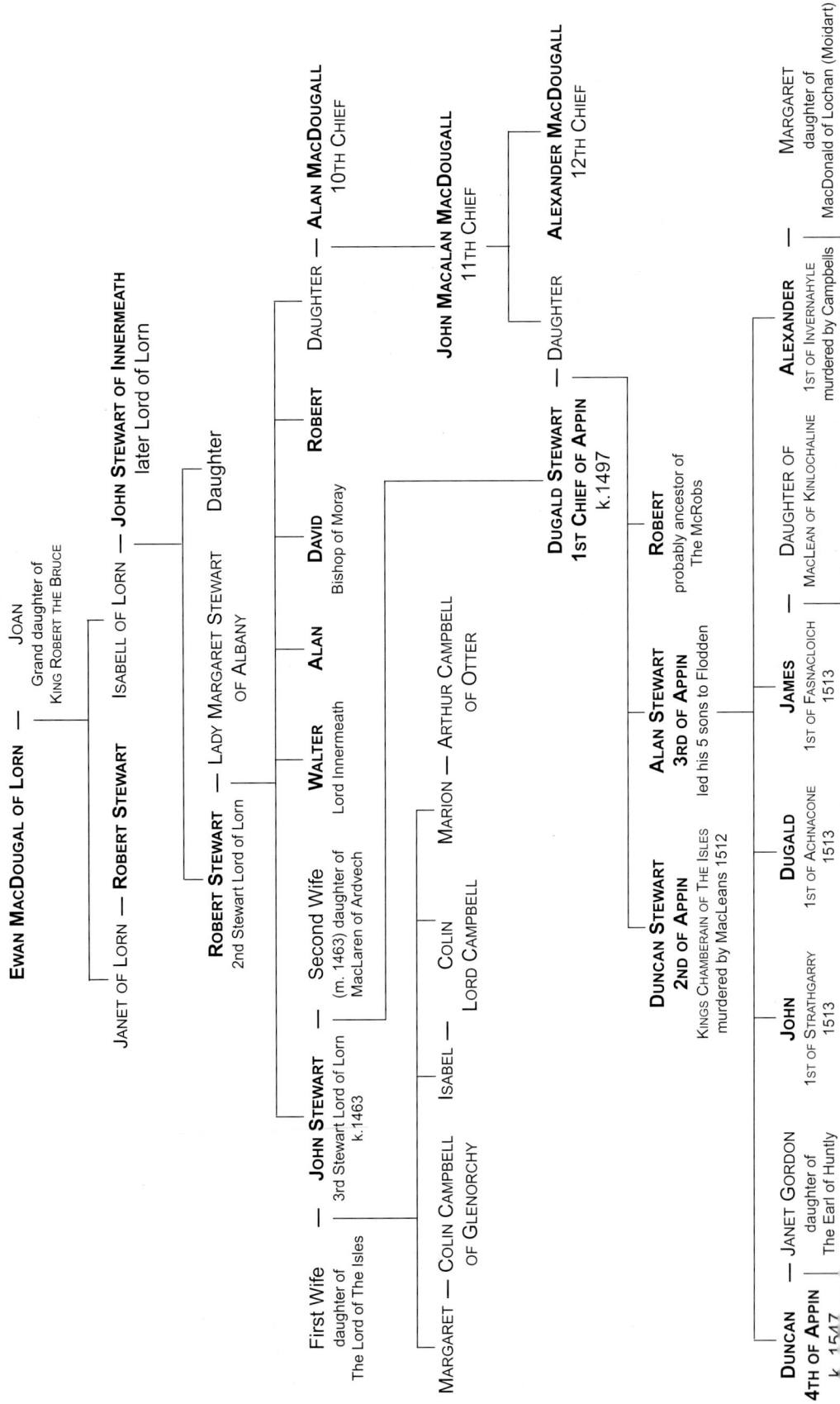

EWAN MACDOUGAL OF LORN — JOAN
Grand daughter of
KING ROBERT THE BRUCE

JANET OF LORN — **ROBERT STEWART**

ISABELL OF LORN — **JOHN STEWART OF INNERMEATH**
later Lord of Lorn

First Wife
daughter of
The Lord of The Isles

— **JOHN STEWART**
3rd Stewart Lord of Lorn
k.1463

Second Wife
(m. 1463) daughter of
MacLaren of Ardvech

ROBERT STEWART — LADY MARGARET STEWART
2nd Stewart Lord of Lorn   OF ALBANY

Daughter

WALTER
Lord Innermeath

ALAN

DAVID
Bishop of Moray

ROBERT

DAUGHTER — **ALAN MACDOUGALL**
10TH CHIEF

MARGARET — COLIN CAMPBELL
OF GLENORCHY

ISABEL —

COLIN
LORD CAMPBELL

MARION — ARTHUR CAMPBELL
OF OTTER

DUGALD STEWART
1ST CHIEF OF APPIN
k.1497

— DAUGHTER

JOHN MACALAN MACDOUGALL
11TH CHIEF

ALEXANDER MACDOUGALL
12TH CHIEF

DUNCAN STEWART
2ND OF APPIN
KINGS CHAMBERAIN OF THE ISLES
murdered by MacLeans 1512

ALAN STEWART
3RD OF APPIN
led his 5 sons to Flodden

ROBERT
probably ancestor of
The McRobs

DUNCAN
4TH OF APPIN
k.1517

— JANET GORDON
daughter of
The Earl of Huntly

JOHN
1ST OF STRATHGARRY
1513

DUGALD
1ST OF ACHNACONE
1513

JAMES
1ST OF FASNACLOICH
1513

DAUGHTER OF
MACLEAN OF KINLOCHALINE

ALEXANDER
1ST OF INVERNAHYLE
murdered by Campbells

MARGARET
daughter of
MacDonald of Lochan (Moidart)

Family Tree (Stewart of Appin / Invernahyle / Ardsheal / Fasnacloich)

- **DAUGHTER OF** Stewart of Bunrannoch

- **DONALD** 2ND OF INVERNAHYLE "Of The Hammers" commanded *Appin Men* at Pinkie 1547 d. 1590

- **HELEN** daughter of Campbell of Dunstaffnage

- **DAUGHTER OF** Duncan Stewart 7th of Appin

- **JOHN**
- **JAMES**
- **DUNCAN** 3RD OF INVERNAHYLE "The Peaceful"

- **DUNCAN** 5TH OF INVERNAHYLE (he had 11 brothers)
- **ALEXANDER** 4TH OF INVERNAHYLE fought under Montrose 1645-46

- **ALEXANDER** 8TH OF INVERNAHYLE fought in 1745-46 battles

- **DONALD** 7TH OF ACHNACONE
- **DUNCAN** killed at Culloden
- **ALEXANDER** killed at Culloden
- **DUGALD** 2ND OF FASNACLOICH
- **NIECE OF** MacDonald of Glencoe
- **JOHN**

- **JOHN** 3RD OF FASNACLOICH
- **DAUGHTER OF** Campbell of Inverawe
- **JOHN** 4TH OF FASNACLOICH

- **JAMES** 8TH OF FASNACLOICH fought in 1745-46

- Decendants in the 20thCentury

- **ELIZABETH STEWART** OF BALLECHIN
- **ANNE CAMPBELL** OF LOCHNELL

- **CHARLES** 5TH OF ARDSHEAL Led clan in 1745-46 d. 1757
- **ISOBEL HALDANE**

- **DUNCAN** 6TH OF ARDSHEAL Estate restored 1781
- **ALEXANDER** d. 1769

- **CHARLES** 7TH OF ARDSHEAL, recognised, 1800 as "Lorn, Appin and Ardsheal"
- **JOHN**

- **LT. COL. DUGALD STEWART** DUTCH ARMY sold Strathgarry circa 1700

- Succesion to **DUNCAN STEWART** OF ACHNACONE d. 1850

- **DUNCAN** 2ND OF ARDSHEAL served with Montrose1644-45
- **JOHN** 3RD OF ARDSHEAL Tutor at Dunkeld 1689
- **JOHN** 4TH OF ARDSHEAL fought at Sheriffmuir

- **MARY** daughter of MacDonald of Keppoch

- **1ST WIFE** DAUGHTER OF CAMPBELL OF LOCHNELL
- **JOHN** 5TH OF APPIN Gordonich bann d. 1595
- **2ND WIFE** DAUGHTER OF MACDONALD OF MOIDART

- **DUNCAN** 6TH OF APPIN
- **JOHN** 1ST OF ARDSHEAL

- **DUNCAN** — **DAUGHTER OF** CAMERON OF LOCHIEL
- **JOHN**
- **ALAN**
- **DAUGHTER**

- **DUNCAN MOR** 8TH OF APPIN joined Montrose 1644, fought at Inverlochy, Auldearn and Kilsyth
- **ALAN** — **DAUGHTER OF** MACLEAN OF COLL
- **DONALD**

- **MARGARET**
- **ROBERT** 9TH OF APPIN joined Dundee, before Killiecrankie with part of the Clan, 1689 fought in 1715 rising
- **DUGALD** 10TH OF APPIN no sons, sold lands in1765, d. 1769

83

Casualties at Culloden

DRAWN FROM "THE STEWARTS OF APPIN" (1880)

Appendix III   List of killed and wounded of the Appin Regiment at the battle of Culloden, copied from
MS. left by Alexander Stewart, Eighth of Invernahyle.

Name	Killed	Wounded
Ardsheal's family -		
John Stewart of Benmore,	1	---
John, son to Alexander Stewart of Acharn,	1	---
James, son to Alexander Stewart of Acharn,	1	---
John Stewart,	1	---
John Stewart,	1	---
William Stewart,	---	1
John Stewart,	1	---
Duncan Stewart, uncle to Ardsheal,	1	---
Dugald Stewart, standard-bearer,	1	---
Alan Mor Stewart,	---	1
William Stewart,	---	1
	8	3
Fasnacloich's family -		
James Stewart, uncle to Fasnacloich,	---	1
James Stewart, younger of Fasnacloich,	---	1
John Stewart, son to Fasnacloich,	---	1
John, son to Duncan Stewart,	---	1
James Stewart, from Ardnamurchan,	1	---
Alan Stewart, son to Ardnamurchan,	1	---
	2	4
Achnacone's family -		
Alexander Stewart, brother to Achnacone,	1	---
Duncan Stewart,	1	---
	2	0
Invernahyle's family -		
Alexander Stewart, son to Ballachelish,	1	---
Duncan, Donald, Dugald, and Alan Stewart, nephews to Ballachelish,	---	4
John Stewart, from Ardnamurchen,	---	1
Charles Stewart, from Bohallie,	---	1
Alexander Stewart, of Invernahyle,	---	1
James Stewart, brotherto Invernahyle,	---	1
Duncan Stewart, from Inverphalla,	---	1
Donald Stewart, from Annat,	---	1
Alan Stewart, died in the East Indies,	---	1
Donald Stewart, nephew to Invernahyle,	1	---
John Stewart, from Balquidder,	1	---
Duncan Stewart,	1	---
John Stewart,	---	1
	4	12

Name	Killed	Wounded
Stewarts, followers of Appin		
Duncan Stewart, from Mull,	1	---
Duncan, Hugh, and John Stewart,		
from Glenlyon,	---	3
John Stewart - Macalan Vane	---	1
John Stewart, alias Macalan,	1	---
Duncan Stewart, *alias* Macalan,	---	1
Malcolm Stewart,	1	---
Dugald Stewart,	1	---
Donald Stewart, natural son to Ballachellan,	1	---
Robert Stewart, natural cousin to Appin,	1	---
Robert Stewart, natural cousin to Appin	---	1
	6	6

Summary of family casualties		
Ardsheal's family,	8	3
Fasnacloich's family,	2	4
Invernahyle's family,	4	12
Achnacone's family,	2	---
Stewarts, followers of Appin,	6	6

Commoners, followers of Appin -		
M'Colls,	18	15
Maclarens,	13	4
Carmichaels,	6	2
M'Combichs,	5	3
M'Intyres,	5	5
M'Innishes, or M'Innises,	4	2
M'Ildeus, or Blacks,	1	---
Mackenzies,	2	3
M'Corquadales,	1	---
M'Uchders,	---	1
Henderson	1	1
M'Rankens,	1	---
M'Cormacks (Buchanans),	5	1
Camerons,	---	1
M'Donalds,	---	1
M'Lachlans,	2	---
MacLeas, or Livingstones,	4	1
M'Arthurs,	1	--
	69	40
Volunteer -		
George Haldane,nephew to Lanrick,		
Ardsheal having married Haldane		
of Lanrick's sister,	1	---
	1	---

Total of killed and wounded,	92	65

Stewart Of Appin Regiment Prisoners

Appendix IV   EXTRACTED FROM "THE PRISONERS OF THE `45"
BY SIR BRUCE GORDON SETON AND JEAN GORDON ARNOT,
SCOTTISH HISTORY SOCIETY 1928

Name	Place of Origin	Eventual Fate, Where Known
John Buchanan	Argyll	Captured at Culloden. Appears to have died in Prison at Tilbury.
Archibald Colquhoun	Appin	Taken at Inverness. Transported 20 March 1747.
Donald Leviston	Appin?	Taken at Culloden. Probably died in prison at Inverness.
John McCallum	Appin	Taken in Appin, May 1746. Discharged, 15 July 1747.*
John McColl, Senior	Appin+	Taken in Appin, May 1746. Discharged, 15 July 1747.*
John McColl, Junior	Appin+	Taken in Appin, May 1746 Discharged, 15 July 1747.*
John McColl	Port-na-Croish,	An officer in the Regiment. Taken Appin to Carlisle. Probably died there, awaiting trial.
Samuel McColl	Appin +	Taken in Appin, May 1746 Discharged 1747.
Samuel McColl	Appin +	Taken in Appin, May 1746 Discharged, 15 April 1747.
Donald McCormick	Appin	Taken August 1746. Sent for trial at Carlisle, but acquitted 19 September 1746. May not have served in the Regiment.
Evan McCulloch	Appin	Taken at Culloden. Probably died of wounds in Inverness.
Samuel McCulloch	Appin	Baggage carrier for Invernahyle. Taken to Carlisle for trial. Appears to have died of scurvy in hospital.
Donald MacDonald	Argyll	Wounded at Prestonpans (in Invernahyle`s Company). Captured in Royal Infirmary, Edinburgh. Tried at Carlisle. Executed at Brampton, 24 October 1746.
Archibald McInnes	Stirlingshire	Arrested Dunblane, 27 April 1746. Seems to have been orderly to a Stewart Officer. Released under General Pardon, 1747.
Duncan McIntyre	Lochielhead	Arrested Inverness, Jun 1746. Transported from Tilbury, March 1747.
Captain Donald MacLaren	Balquidder	Captured, wounded, in Braes of Leny, July 1746. Made a daring escape on way to trial in Carlisle, throwing himself over the cliff of Annandale`s Beefstand (now MacLaren`s Leap). Returned to Invernantie and lived in disguise until the Act of Indemnity.

Name	Place of Origin	Eventual Fate, Where Known
Allan Stewart	Doune, but served in Appin`s	Taken in Inverness, June 1746. Probably died in captivity at Tilbury.
Dougal Stewart	Appin	Wounded at Prestonpans. Captured in hospital. Discharge 17 April 1747.
Duncan Stewart	Argyll	Taken Inverness, June 1746. Transported, 31 March 1747.
James Stewart	Appin	Said to be a natural brother of Ardshiel`s. Quartermaster of Appin Regiment. Helped senior officers to escape. Condemned to death, but ,reprieved for saving life of a Campbell Officer, was transported.
John Stewart	Glencoe	Taken at Larbert, 8 February 1746. Discharged, 1 January 1747.
John Stewart	Ballachulish	Wounded at Prestonpans, captured in hospital. Released under General Pardon, 1747.
Lieutenant William Stewart	Appin?	Probably the William, cousin of Ardshiel`s. Captured, wounded, March 1746. Transported.
Possibly Alexander Scot	Perthshire	Listed as possibly "Stewart" Regiment. Captured at Carlisle. Sentenced to death, October 1746, but pardoned on condition of enlistment, 22 July 1748. This man was almost certainly of Roy Stuart`s Regiment, which left detachments at Carlisle, while the Stewarts of Appin did not.
John Livingston	Ardnamurchan	From his district of origin, he may well have been an Appin Livingston, but he is listed as having served in Glengyle`s Regiment. He was released, 21 August 1747.

* *The frequent releases on this date were due to the Act of General Pardon of 1747.*

+ *The four McColls, taken in May 1746, at or near their homes in Appin, might well have escaped capture if two of them had not tried to raid supplies or cattle from the Argyll Militia camp, the night before their arrests.*

SUMMARY OF FATE OF ALL THE PRISONERS			
Executed	120	Escaped from Prison	58
Died in Prison	88	Released or exchanged	1,287
(Government Figures)		Conditional pardon	76
Transported	936	Fate unknown	684
Banished	222	*(many of whom died in prison)*	

Appendix V *The Battle of Culloden* – FIELD POSITIONS, (SIMPLIFIED) AT THE BEGINNING OF BATTLE

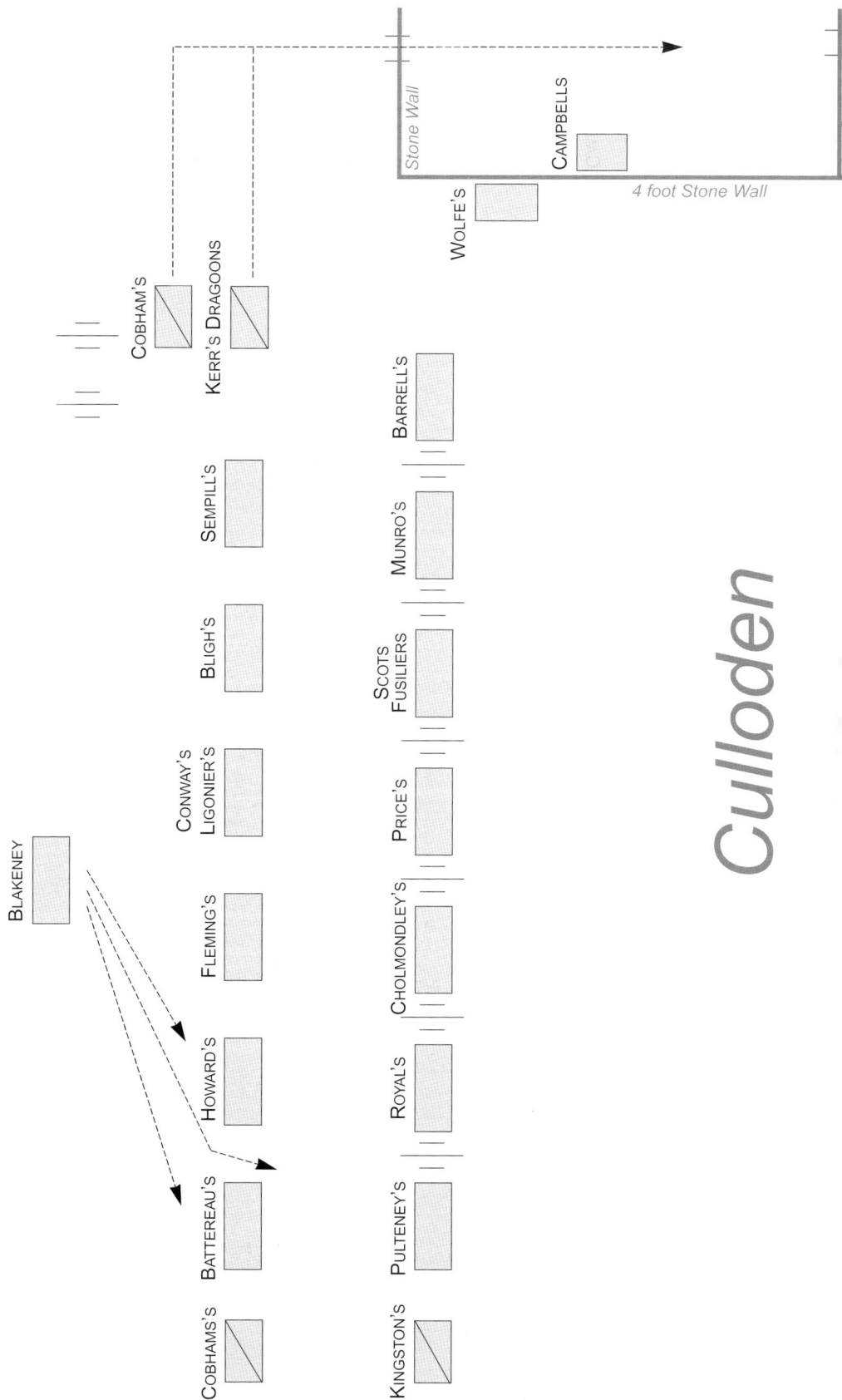

COBHAM'S

KINGSTON'S

BLAKENEY

BATTEREAU'S

PULTENEY'S

FLEMING'S

HOWARD'S

ROYAL'S

CONWAY'S
LIGONIER'S

CHOLMONDLEY'S

BLIGH'S

PRICE'S

SEMPILL'S

SCOTS
FUSILIERS

MUNRO'S

COBHAM'S

KERR'S DRAGOONS

BARRELL'S

Stone Wall

WOLFE'S

CAMPBELLS

4 foot Stone Wall

Culloden

CAMPBELLS

Sunken track

ATHOLL

CAMERONS

STEWARTS OF APPIN

FRASERS

CLAN CHATTAN

MACLACHLANS AND
MACLEANS

FARQUARSONS
[and others]

ROY STEWART

CLANRANALD

KEPPOCH

GLENGARRY

OGILVY

GORDON OF
AVOCHIE

LEWIS GORDON

GLENBUCHAT

PERTH

SCOTS ROYAL

IRISH PICQUETS

FITZJAMES
AND ELCHO

BALMERINO

THE PRINCE

KILMARNOCK AND
PITSLIGO
[Dismounted]

Field
(Simplified)

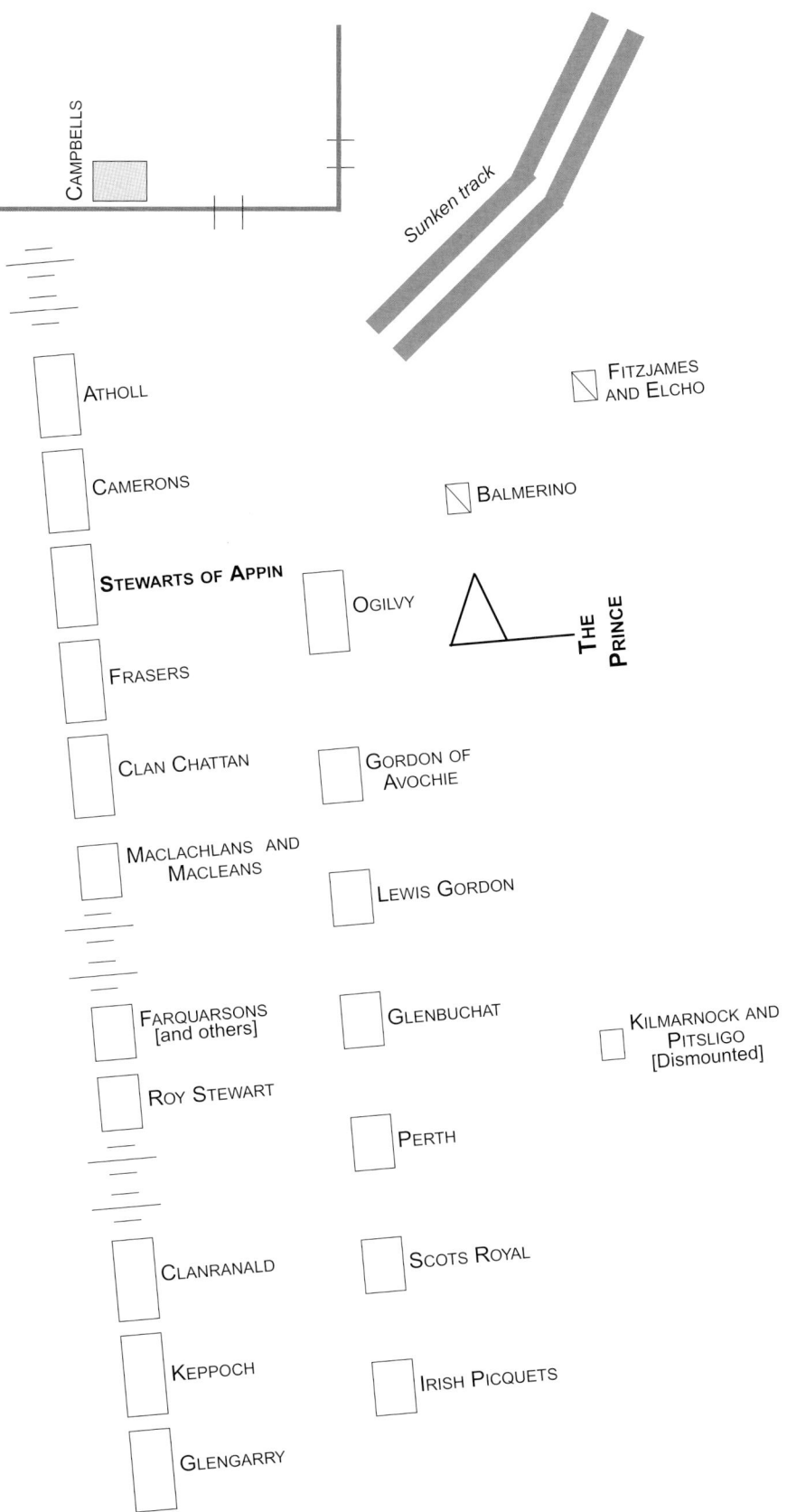

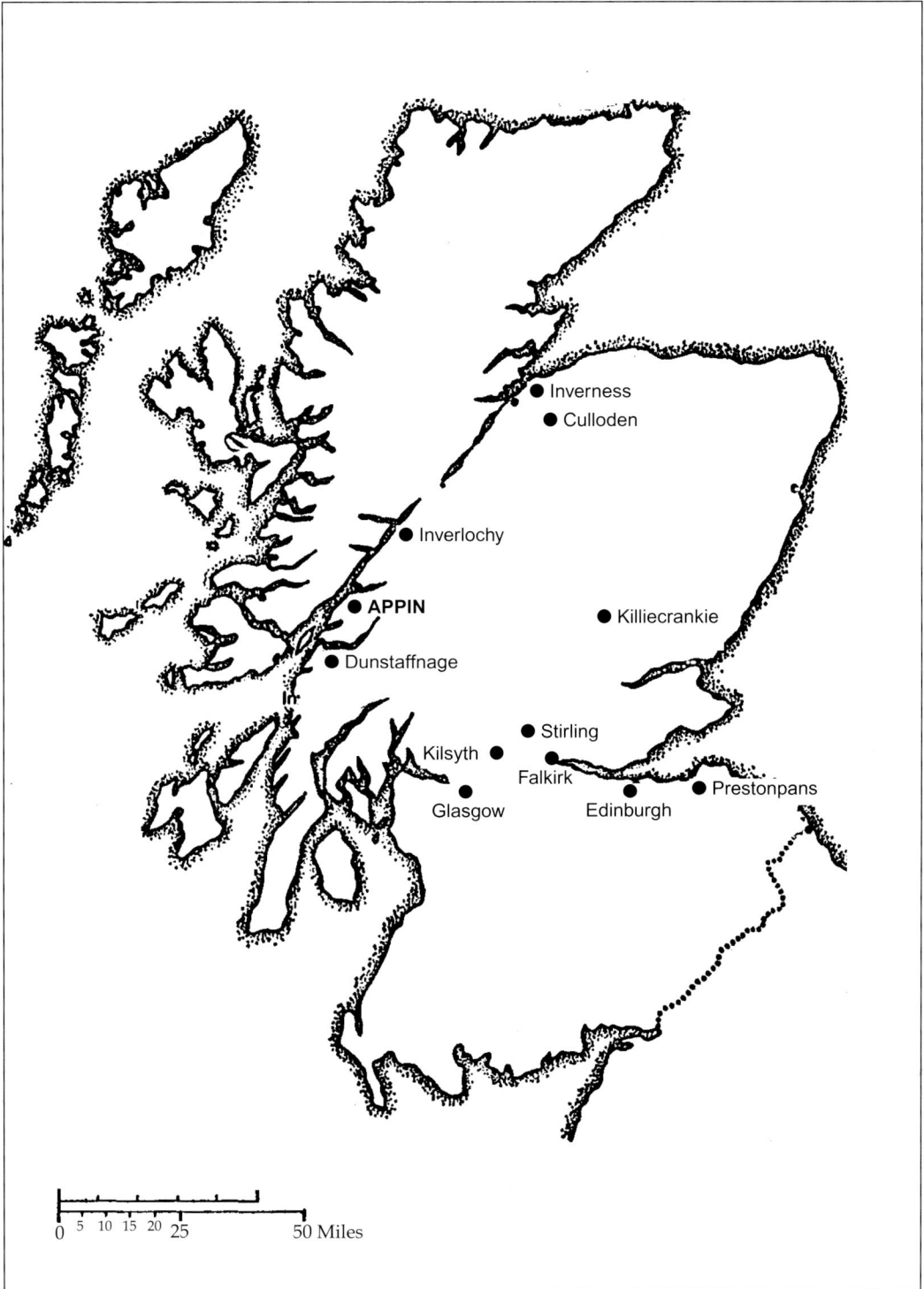

Inverness

Culloden

Inverlochy

APPIN

Killiecrankie

Dunstaffnage

Stirling

Kilsyth

Falkirk

Prestonpans

Glasgow

Edinburgh

0 5 10 15 20 25   50 Miles

Scotland of the Stewarts

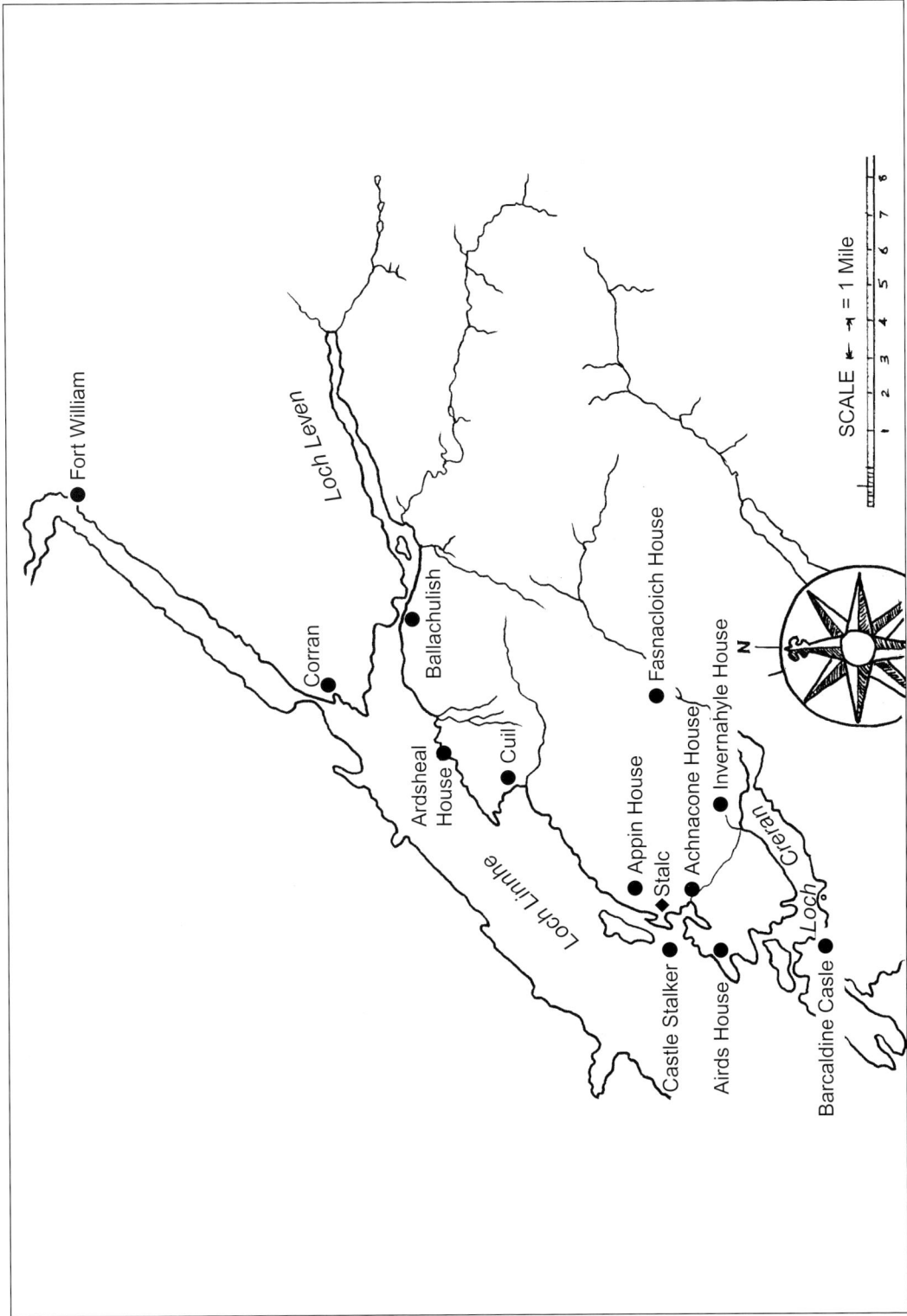

Fort William

Loch Leven

Corran

Ballachulish

Ardsheal House

Cuil

Appin House

Stalc

Castle Stalker

Airds House

Achnacone House

Fasnacloich House

Invernahyle House

Loch Creran

Barcaldine Casle

Loch Linnhe

N

SCALE ⟵ ⟶ = 1 Mile

1 2 3 4 5 6 7 8